AMERICA'S UNTAPPED RESOURCE

AMERICA'S UNTAPPED RESOURCE

Low-Income Students in Higher Education

RICHARD D. KAHLENBERG, EDITOR

THE CENTURY FOUNDATION PRESS ◆ NEW YORK

The Century Foundation sponsors and supervises timely analyses of economic policy, foreign affairs, and domestic political issues. Not-for-profit and nonpartisan, it was founded in 1919 and endowed by Edward A. Filene.

LIBRARY OF CONGRESS CATALOGING-IN-PUBLICATION DATA

America's untapped resource : low-income students in higher education /
Richard D. Kahlenberg, editor.
     p. cm.
   Includes bibliographical references and index.
   ISBN 0-87078-485-4 (pbk. : alk. paper)
   1. People with social disabilities--Education (Higher) --United States.
2. Poor--Education (Higher) --United States. 3. Education, Higher--United States--Costs. 4. Universities and colleges--United States--Admission. I. Kahlenberg,
Richard D. II. Century Foundation.III. Title.
   LC4823.A54 2004
   378.1'986'942--dc22
                                                            2003023798

Manufactured in the United States of America.

FOREWORD

The American ideal of a meritocracy, where one can advance as far as talent permits, remains a cherished national goal. While any sensible person recognizes that reality falls far short of perfection in this regard, it is a staple of political discourse that there is steady progress toward the ideal. But is the long-term trend as favorable as it once was? Are there warning signs in the significant increases in income and wealth inequality over the past thirty years?

In the United States, at least, a single characteristic—access to and success in higher education—turns out to have enormous implications for one's economic prospects in life. While stories of rags to riches and high school dropouts who made it big are certainly fascinating, they have very little to do with statistical reality. Without a college education, one is much more likely to have average or below-average income and wealth. The good news is that a larger percentage of our young attend institutions of higher education than do those in almost all other countries. But the overall numbers may obscure a more troubling truth: the share of high school graduates going on to college varies dramatically according to family income. Within two years of graduating from high school, two-thirds from the wealthiest quartile enter a four-year college, compared to one-fifth from the poorest quartile. In addition, at the elite schools that are most closely associated with financial and career success, these correlations are even higher. Nearly three-quarters of students enrolled at the most selective 146 colleges are from the top economic quartile, compared with just 3 percent from the bottom economic quartile. There is, moreover, another disparity that belongs in any discussion of how to create a more level playing field in terms of college opportunities.

For while there has been some improvement, there remain sharp differences along racial and ethnic lines in terms of access to higher education. Only about one-quarter of African American males, for example, enter a four-year college in the fall following their graduation from high school.

For a long time, the cost of higher education together with the reality of favoritism for children of alumni and restrictions or outright bars on applicants from various ethnic and religious groups meant that private higher education was largely confined to the "rich and the well born." The growth of public higher education in the Midwest and the West, however, did much to expand the pool from which undergraduates were drawn. The vast expansion of opportunity symbolized by the 8 million college enrollees using the GI Bill after World War II was another important development in breaking down barriers. Today, while college costs vary tremendously, access is in general much more broadly available than in the past. But higher education is still far from universal, with just one-quarter of the U.S. population over the age of twenty-five holding a four-year college degree.

Starting with support for student loans in the 1950s and continuing with later programs, especially the 1965 Higher Education Act, federal policy came to reflect a national commitment to providing college opportunities for students of all backgrounds. In recent years, this focus on expanding the pool of college students has become blurred, as public policy at the federal, state, and university level drifted, often placing an emphasis on subsidizing middle-class families rather than reaching those students who, but for financial aid, would not attend college. Policymakers also have tended to be shortsighted in terms of their goals, relying too heavily on merely getting students in the door rather than providing the support to make sure they graduate. And our most selective private colleges probably have spent too little energy ensuring that students from poor and working-class families can partake in the excellent education they offer.

To take a fresh look at these questions, The Century Foundation commissioned papers by some of the leading figures writing about higher education today: Lawrence E. Gladieux, an education consultant formerly with the College Board; P. Michael Timpane, former president of Teachers College, Columbia University, now at the Aspen Institute; Arthur M. Hauptman, a longtime education consultant;

Anthony P. Carnevale of the Educational Testing Service; and Stephen J. Rose of ORC Macro. The volume also includes an appendix on the percentage of low-income students at top American colleges prepared by Donald E. Heller of Pennsylvania State University. It was edited by Century Foundation senior fellow Richard D. Kahlenberg.

The Century Foundation has long been committed to publishing works on equal opportunity in education. Our education task force reports include *Making the Grade*, examining federal elementary and secondary education policy in the early 1980s; *Facing the Challenge*, an analysis of school governance issues in the early 1990s; and *Divided We Fail*, published in 2002, which outlines ways to create economically and racially integrated schools through public school choice. Our recent education books include *Hard Lessons: Public Schools and Privatization*, by Carol Ascher, Norm Fruchter, and Robert Berne; Richard Rothstein's *The Way We Were? The Myths and Realities of America's Student Achievement*; Kahlenberg's *All Together Now: Creating Middle-Class Schools through Public School Choice*; and Joan Lombardi's *Time to Care: Redesigning Child Care to Promote Education, Support Families, and Build Communities*. We also have published a series of collected essays on education, notably *A Notion at Risk: Preserving Public Education as an Engine for Social Mobility*, edited by Kahlenberg; *Raising Standards or Raising Barriers? Inequality and High-Stakes Testing in Public Education*, edited by Gary Orfield and Mindy L. Kornhaber; and *Public School Choice vs. Private School Vouchers*, also edited by Kahlenberg. We have an ongoing project on school financing by Richard Rothstein and James Guthrie as well.

American higher education remains a global leader from almost every standpoint. The nation's colleges are a magnet for some of the brightest young people in the world. We rely heavily, in fact, on foreign students to be part of our pool of workers, scientists, inventors, and physicians. And, as noted above, economic studies show that higher education adds vastly to a person's productivity and earnings potential. In other words, college in America is a great prize, nothing short of a gateway to the American dream. Thus, at a time when, if anything, inequality appears to be on the increase again, the fundamental question posed by the essays in this volume remains of great importance: What must we do to make higher education more available to those who face special barriers to entrance and graduation? Until we effectively answer that question, the dream of a true meritocracy will remain unfulfilled.

On behalf of the Trustees of The Century Foundation, I thank the contributors for their valuable efforts.

Richard C. Leone, President
The Century Foundation
January 2004

CONTENTS

INTRODUCTION

Richard D. Kahlenberg

American higher education is in a state of flux as Congress and the Bush administration begin discussions over the reauthorization of the Higher Education Act and universities react to a landmark U.S. Supreme Court ruling on affirmative action. State legislatures are debating tuition levels and the role of merit versus need-based aid, and institutions are evaluating early decision plans and the proper role of a newly redesigned Scholastic Assessment Test (SAT). This volume takes stock of these events with a particular focus on how these controversies affect the groups least well served by current higher education policies: poor and working-class students of all racial and ethnic groups.

The introduction outlines the extent of the problem low-income and working-class students face in higher education and provides an overview of the three essays that constitute the bulk of this volume: a discussion of federal, state, and institutional financial aid policies by former College Board official Lawrence E. Gladieux; a chapter on profound problems in academic preparation, performance, and "persistence" (meaning the ability to stay the course until graduation) among low-income students in postsecondary institutions written by P. Michael Timpane of the Aspen Institute and Arthur M. Hauptman, an education consultant; and a chapter on affirmative action policies for low-income students, as well as minority students, at selective universities by Anthony P. Carnevale of the Educational Testing Service and Stephen J. Rose of ORC Macro International. The volume concludes with an appendix prepared by Donald E. Heller of

Pennsylvania State University, which shows significant variation in the percentages of low-income and working-class students at the nation's 146 most selective colleges.

UNEQUAL PARTICIPATION AND PERSISTENCE IN HIGHER EDUCATION

Low-income students face three major inequalities in higher education: they go to college in fewer instances than others; they complete college at lower rates; they attend four-year colleges generally, and selective schools particularly, with substantially less frequency. As the chapters in this volume demonstrate, low-income students drop out of high school five times as often as high-income students (21 percent vs. 4 percent). Two of every three students from the top socioeconomic quartile enroll in a four-year institution within two years of high school graduation, compared with one in five from the bottom quartile. Within five years of beginning postsecondary education, 41 percent from the richest quartile but just 6 percent from the poorest quartile receive a bachelor's degree. Of all college first-year entrants, almost half of low-income students attend two-year community colleges, in contrast with just one in ten high-income students. At top-tier colleges, students in the highest socioeconomic quartile take up 74 percent of the available slots, compared with 3 percent from the bottom quartile.[1] Indeed, the underrepresentation of low-income students at elite colleges is many times greater than it is for "underrepresented minorities," who are the subject of the wars over affirmative action.

Inequality in access matters a great deal because of the growing wage premium provided by a college education generally and because of the particular advantages of attending a selective university. As Gladieux notes, the median annual household income in 1999 was roughly $36,000 for those with a high school degree, $64,000 for those with a bachelor's degree, and $100,000 for those with a professional degree, a spread that is now much greater than it once was. Which college a student attends also makes a difference. While community colleges are advertised as a gateway to four-year colleges, less than one-tenth of community college students ultimately receive a bachelor's degree. Carnevale and Rose point out that there are three major advantages to attending a selective four-year college. Controlling for test scores, students in selective colleges are more likely to graduate. Of students scoring between 1000 and 1100 on the SAT, for example, 86 percent graduate from the most selective colleges, compared to only 67 percent from the least selective. Attending a top-tier college promotes access to postgraduate schools as well. Among students scoring above 1200 on the SAT, 48 percent of those attending selective colleges go on to attend graduate school, as opposed to 26 percent of those attending less competitive and noncompetitive schools. Though more controversial, a number of studies also show a wage premium of 5–20 percent representing the value added from attending a competitive school (controlling for initial ability). Even studies that find only a small wage premium on average reveal that low-income students gain disproportionately from attending a more selective school.

FINANCIAL AID IN HIGHER EDUCATION

Students from less fortunate circumstances are less likely to attend college in part because they are not as well prepared on average (see discussion below), but inadequate financial aid presents a significant independent barrier. As Gladieux remarks, "The least bright rich kids have as much chance of going to college as the smartest poor kids." Spiraling tuition costs, coupled with growing income inequality, mean that the average price of attending a public four-year college represents nearly 60 percent of annual income for low-income families, 16 percent for middle-income families, and 5 percent for high-income families—"sticker shock" that discourages many students of modest means from even considering higher education. After factoring in financial aid packages, Gladieux notes that "unmet need"—the price of attending minus financial aid and family's ability to pay—is considerably higher for low-income students than others. To make up the shortfall, such students must take on greater debt and work longer hours. Working one's way through college is a time-honored tradition in America, but studies find that at a certain point now being reached by many students, work overwhelms studies and discourages youths from graduating, leaving many with large debts and no degrees.

Originally, federal financial aid policies were meant to focus on the problems of the poor for a very simple reason. Because college offers enormous potential financial rewards to individuals who have the opportunity to attend, and because a relatively small proportion (one-quarter) of Americans have four-year degrees, publicly supported financial aid was justified mainly as a way to encourage students who would not otherwise be able to attend. Higher education can be considered in large measure a public good—all benefit when the society as a whole is more highly educated—so the larger community has an interest in targeting aid on those who are on the verge of deciding to attend but would attend only with outside assistance. By contrast, public subsidies for those who would attend with or without aid are much more difficult to justify since they essentially constitute a transfer of wealth from the general taxpaying public to a small elite. As Gladieux points out, the "but for such aid" principle was at the center of the original Higher Education Act of 1965 and the Pell Grants (which soon followed), steering grants specifically to low-income students. Since then, state and national policies have taken three giant steps away from that principle, he finds, steps facilitated by members of both political parties.

First came a shift in federal financial aid funding from grants for the poor to loans for the middle class as well as the poor. Twenty years ago the mix was 55 percent grants, 41 percent loans. Today the reverse holds true, with loans accounting for 58 percent and grants 41 percent. The prospect of debt appears to discourage many low-income students who otherwise might aspire to and qualify for higher education. The shift toward loans diverts scarce resources from the poor and working-class to a much larger group of less needy beneficiaries.

Second, on the state level, there was a shift from need-based to non-need based merit scholarships. Beginning with the 1993 HOPE (Helping Outstanding Pupils Educationally) Scholarship, created by Georgia Democratic governor Zell Miller, states adopted scholarships for high-achieving students, not so much as a way of increasing the overall number of students going on to higher education but as a method of trying to keep bright students in state—a kind of internal trade barrier between states. States also adopted so-called 529 plans to encourage tax-free savings for college—again benefiting the better-off more than the needy.

Third, the Clinton administration pushed the expansion of education tax breaks during the late 1990s. Although Clinton's Treasury secretary, Robert Rubin, argued that increasing scholarships would provide a more efficient and better-targeted way of expanding access to higher education, the political argument—that tax breaks can accomplish social good while "reducing the size of government"—prevailed.[2] The plans flipped the original logic of the Higher Education Act, benefiting middle- and upper-middle-income families disproportionately and the neediest the least. Not surprisingly, a recent study found no evidence that such tax breaks increased access to postsecondary education.[3] The Bush administration and Congress have broadened Clinton's tax incentives, extending them further up the income ladder and expanding the amount of tax-favored college savings allowed.

Meanwhile, colleges are beginning to act less like nonprofit educational institutions and more like market players, using aid as a way of attracting talented students away from competitor universities rather than as a method of helping those who need it most. Despite some high-profile examples to the contrary, universities as a whole have increasingly relied on early admissions decisions, which hurt less fortunate students who cannot commit early to any particular college because they needed to compare aid packages.[4]

Gladieux suggests a number of important steps to restore the need-based principle of financial aid. His central recommendation is to restore Pell Grant funding to the purchasing power it had in the late 1970s. Pell Grants are highly targeted, with 90 percent of benefits going to students with parental or personal incomes below $40,000.[5] Current annual Pell Grant funding stands at about $11 billion; restoring its purchasing power to earlier levels would cost an additional $12–15 billion.

The annual price tag of Gladieux's proposal—roughly $25 billion—seems high until one considers the far less defensible yet massive subsidies currently provided to the better-off. State governments fund public colleges at a rate that exceeds $50 billion annually (tuition covers only 19 percent of costs of public higher education), which helps out many who could afford to pay more. Indeed, at flagship public universities, the beneficiaries of taxpayer largesse are actually wealthier on average than those attending private colleges.[6] Federal tax breaks for higher education are expected to cost $60 billion over the next five years. Federal loans stand at $39 billion, almost four times the current size of Pell Grants, with a cost to taxpayers of $2 billion annually. Gladieux argues for making Pell Grants an entitlement, on par with tax breaks, which are not limited by the annual appropriations process. Restoring the historic value of the Pell Grant and making it an entitlement is not only equitable; it also provides the maximum societal payoff—helping primarily those who might not go to college at all without the program.

Gladieux's other recommendations include:

*   Offering tuition tax breaks to the poor and working-class. If our
    society is going to insist on funneling financial aid to the well-off
    through the tax code, we should provide comparable relief for
    the poor through refundable tax credits or matching deposits for
    nest egg savings.

*   Returning to need-based scholarships over merit-based scholar-
    ships.

*   Providing better publicity about aid programs. Surveys find that
    students and families—particularly those with few resources—
    significantly overestimate the cost of college and underestimate
    the amount of aid available.

It must be acknowledged that a rising chorus of critics has raised
an important objection to the type of approach Gladieux backs,
charging that augmenting federal aid merely encourages colleges to
increase prices or to displace their own institutional aid for disadvantaged students, leaving the poor no better off. These critics say
that as the competition for top students has increased, many universities respond to increases in federal aid for the disadvantaged
by shifting their own assistance to need-blind merit programs. In
this way, aid for poor students is transformed, in essence, into public charity for institutions. Gladieux rejects this hypothesis, though it
appears that at the very least more research is needed to sort out
the competing empirical claims. He also rejects calls for government
legislation capping college costs but says colleges themselves should
do a better job of containing costs and making their finances more
transparent.

ENABLING LOW-INCOME STUDENTS TO
SUCCEED IN COLLEGE

Timpane and Hauptman complement the important discussion of
broad-based participation in college (in terms of initial enrollment)
by outlining what they call the other "three p's": how thoroughly

low-income students are prepared for college, how well they perform in college, and how often they persist to graduation.

While it is true that serious shortfalls of financial aid block some students' aspirations, Timpane and Hauptman say, the problems for disadvantaged students go deeper. They are less academically prepared for college than middle-class students. SAT scores of low-income students lag two hundred points behind high-income students on average, and a U.S. Department of Education survey found that only one-fifth of low-income students, compared with nearly three-fifths of high-income students, are "highly qualified" for college. While there is little reliable data on the performance of low-income students in college, surveys find that such students are six times less likely to graduate with a bachelor's degree than high-income students. The United States is generally much more successful at getting students into college than graduating them—less than half who enroll in a higher education program receive a degree in that program— and the college dropout problem is particularly prevalent for students from poorer backgrounds.

Timpane and Hauptman recommend three sets of policy changes. In order to better prepare low-income students in elementary and secondary school, the authors call on institutions of higher learning to reassert their historic role in lending their talents to shape K–12 education. Whereas university leaders once set the basic high school curriculum (through the Committee of Twelve), and Harvard president James Conant helped promote the comprehensive high school structure, in recent years elementary and secondary education has often been held in disdain by the academy, a disdain symbolized by the low prestige conferred on schools of education. Business leaders have largely replaced college presidents as the instigators of K–12 school reform. The authors urge colleges to take a special role in training teachers to meet the needs of low-income students and to form so-called K–16 partnerships with disadvantaged primary and secondary schools that are far more ambitious and consequential than those that have sprouted in the past twenty years.

To strengthen the transition from high school to college, Timpane and Hauptman call for correcting the "lopsided" manner in which the federal government favors financial aid resources over support for programs aimed at academic preparation. The federal government's two leading early intervention programs, TRIO and GEAR-UP (Gaining Early Awareness and Readiness for Undergraduate Programs), are funded at 5 percent, and less than 1 percent, respectively, of what is allocated yearly for financial aid. TRIO, which since 1965 has established higher education information centers in poor communities, has identified talented high school students from poor families, and has offered mentoring and advice, remains a demonstration project, reaching only 10 percent of those eligible. GEAR-UP, which since 1998 has sought to build on the TRIO idea to create mentoring and tutoring partnerships between colleges and businesses and high-poverty middle schools, also is underfunded. While the program is still being formally evaluated, its counterpart in the private sector—Eugene Lang's "I Have a Dream" plan—has been highly successful. Timpane and Hauptman call for greatly expanding TRIO and GEAR-UP to reach most, if not all, eligible students.

Timpane and Hauptman also believe colleges can smooth the transition from high school by tying admissions standards to K–12 standards adopted by states. Today, colleges admit students based on SAT and ACT[7] scores and grades rather than on the basis of performance on state assessments tied to state standards. The newly redesigned SAT is a small step in the right direction, but much greater alignment is required. In their most radical recommendation, Timpane and Hauptman call for a comprehensive review of the joint responsibility of K–12 and higher education to provide remedial training for college entrants needing it and for abolishing tuition requirements when colleges provide such training. "Perhaps the most objectionable aspect of current student aid policy," they argue, is the practice of requiring students to borrow "substantial funds to finance the acquisition of skills that they should have received for free in K–12 education."

Finally, Timpane and Hauptman stress better support programs once students are in college and, like Gladieux, urge more targeted aid so that low-income students do not drop out or stretch themselves thin with full-time workloads. In addition, they advocate allocating state and federal aid to institutions at least in part based on how many students advance or graduate in the spring rather than on how many enroll in the fall. The emphasis on performance and persistence (not just participation) in higher education in some ways parallels the emphasis on standards and accountability (not just per-pupil expenditure) that has swept through primary and secondary education. This effort must be pursued carefully so as not to penalize deserving students.

AFFIRMATIVE ACTION FOR LOW-INCOME STUDENTS AT ELITE INSTITUTIONS

While affirmative action programs have focused on the important issue of creating racially integrated student bodies in selective colleges, Carnevale and Rose find that universities provide no comparable help to low-income students, the claims of university officials notwithstanding. The underrepresentation of the poor and working-class at elite universities is far greater than the underrepresentation of racial minorities; indeed, today, the former are found there as infrequently as the latter would be if affirmative action programs had been eliminated and replaced by a regime of grades and test scores.[8] Economically disadvantaged students are twenty-five times less likely to be found on elite college campuses than affluent students—and yet this phenomenon receives none of the attention or moral outrage associated with efforts to curtail racial preferences.[9]

Most universities say they already provide a leg up to disadvantaged applicants and would admit more low-income students if these applicants could handle the work. In their amicus brief in the University of Michigan affirmative action cases, eight elite universities said they "already give significant favorable consideration" to socioeconomic status.[10] The former presidents of Princeton and Harvard, William Bowen and Derek Bok, argue in their seminal book, *The Shape of the River,* that it is not "realistic" to admit more disadvantaged students: "The problem is not that poor but qualified candidates go undiscovered, but that there are simply too few of these candidates in the first place."[11]

The stunning conclusion of the Carnevale and Rose chapter is that this conventional wisdom is dead wrong on both fronts. If low-income students routinely received a break in admissions, as many colleges suggest they do, one would expect to see them overrepresented with regard to their academic records. (Racial preferences, for example, boost black and Latino percentages from 4 percent at the nation's top 146 colleges under a system of grades and test scores to 12 percent.) In fact, the proportion of poor and working-class students today is lower, not higher, than it would be if grades and test scores were the sole basis for admissions, the researchers discover.[12] The finding tracks with a study of law school admissions, which reveals that, despite the rhetoric of admissions committees, law schools give no leg up to disadvantaged applicants.[13] Growing evidence suggests not only

that colleges provide preferences to the offspring of (mostly affluent) alumni but also that they provide a leg up to "development"
candidates—those whose parents provide a sizable donation to the
university.[14]

In fact, selective universities could admit far more low-income
students than they currently do with no drop in graduation rates,
Carnevale and Rose conclude. "There are large numbers of students
from families with low-income and low levels of parental education
who are academically prepared for bachelor's degree attainment, even
in the most selective colleges," they write. Only 44 percent of low-
income students who score in the top quartile academically attend a
four-year college, and this group constitutes "low-hanging fruit" for
selective schools.

For the top 146 colleges, as defined by Barron's guide to colleges,
Carnevale and Rose simulated a pool consisting of all students who
have good grades and score above 1300 on the SAT (or the ACT
equivalent), plus economically disadvantaged students with high grades
and test scores (between 1000 and 1300 on the SAT). Students were
considered disadvantaged if they were in the bottom 40 percent by
socioeconomic status (defined according to parents' income, education, and occupation) or attended high schools with a high percentage
of students eligible for free and reduced-price lunch or with a low percentage of high school graduates. Carnevale and Rose's model assumes
that all students within the pool created—disadvantaged students with
1000–1300 SAT scores plus all students who score between 1300 and
1600—have an equal chance of admissions.[15] The 1000-level cutoff is
employed because students have a good chance of succeeding when
they score above that point. The authors estimate that the socioeconomic preference implied under the model is roughly half the extent of
that currently used for race. The top 146 colleges represent the most
selective 10 percent of four-year colleges and are at the heart of the
debate over affirmative action policies, which currently are used primarily at the top 20 percent of four-year institutions.[16]

Colleges admitting from this pool would have far more economic
diversity—roughly 38 percent from lower economic half compared
with 10 percent today—yet, if colleges also eliminated legacy and
athletic preferences, overall academic quality would not suffer at all.
To the contrary, graduation rates would actually climb, from 86 percent now to almost 90 percent. One reason for confidence in this
simulation is that economic affirmative action is not meant to be a

challenge to merit but rather a better approximation of it. A 3.6 grade point average and SAT of 1200 surely means something more for a low-income-household, first-generation college applicant who attended terrible schools than for a student whose parents have graduate degrees and pay for the finest private schooling. There also is some evidence that a student who has done well despite having to overcome serious obstacles is likely to have greater long-run potential. One study of Harvard students in the 1950s, 1960s, and 1970s found that blue-collar students with more modest SAT scores were the most successful of all as adults.[17]

The appendix to this volume compiled by Donald Heller suggests that many selective schools could admit greater numbers of low-income and working-class students and still maintain very high standards. Heller looks at the percentage of students receiving Pell Grants as a proxy for economic diversity, noting that 90 percent of all dependent Pell Grant recipients at four-year colleges come from roughly the bottom 40 percent of the economic distribution. In the 2001–2002 academic year, Pell recipients constituted 32 percent of students at University of California, Berkeley and 24 percent at Smith—levels several times higher than Bowen's Princeton (7 percent) or Bok's Harvard (7 percent). In Bowen and Bok's pessimistic view of how well poor and working-class students can perform, one may detect shadows of Conant's reservations about the GI Bill, which he thought would overpopulate higher education with underqualified students.[18]

These findings about the desirability of economic affirmative action are highly significant in their own right, but they are directly relevant to the ongoing debate over racial affirmative action as well. Carnevale and Rose welcome the Supreme Court's support of race-sensitive admissions at the University of Michigan Law School in *Grutter v. Bollinger* and argue that racial preferences should continue, alongside a new system of economic preferences, for reasons of fairness, diversity, and politics. Racial discrimination, they note, remains an obstacle to student performance. Housing discrimination helps explain in particular why low-income African Americans and Latinos are more likely than similarly situated whites to attend schools with high concentrations of poverty, a substantial obstacle to superior performance. Using race directly is the best guarantee of producing a diverse class, they say, because most alternatives, including economic affirmative action, result in at least a modest drop in minority admissions. As a matter of politics, the important policy goal of promoting economic affirmative action is more likely to be acceptable if it is offered as a supplement to, rather than a substitute for, racial affirmative action, they say. This certainly seems true among progressives. When liberals say they oppose class-based affirmative action because "it will end up helping a lot of poor whites and Asians," presumably if the policy were put in place on top of race-specific affirmative action, they would see aiding poor whites and Asians as a desirable goal.

Now that the Supreme Court has put race-sensitive admissions on solid legal footing—at least for the next twenty-five years—one can hope that universities will take on the larger issue of economic diversity, as Carnevale and Rose urge. Higher education must resist the temptation to declare victory in the affirmative action wars and consider the job of addressing inequality to have been completed.

It is clear that race-sensitive admissions alone will not provide a level playing field. In the University of Michigan undergraduate case, *Gratz v. Bollinger*, Justice Ruth Bader Ginsburg, joined by Justices David Souter and Stephen Breyer, supported affirmative action with data finding that African Americans and Hispanics have higher poverty rates than whites (22.1 percent and 21.2 percent vs. 7.5 percent) and that black and Latino students "are all too often educated in poverty-stricken and underperforming institutions."[19] But, in practice, affirmative action in higher education does little to reach these low-income and working-class minority students. Bowen and Bok, strong supporters of affirmative action, found that 86 percent of blacks who enrolled in the twenty-eight selective universities they studied were middle or upper-middle class.[20] And race-based programs do nothing to help students from white and Asian families living in poverty or attending "poverty-stricken and underperforming institutions."

Bok argues that a wealthy Harvard minority student is not admitted as a matter of fairness or reparations but because he or she adds to the student body.[21] The whole concept of "deserving" or "earning" a spot is considered naive by many members of the academy. Students are admitted because they fit the needs of the university and the society at a particular point in time, not because there is anything intrinsically worthy about them.[22] Carnevale and Rose's polling data, however, suggest that Americans are deeply invested in the notion that higher education is a ticket to opportunity, and students should be judged by merit—achievements in light of whether one worked hard to overcome economic obstacles. For most Americans, students are not admitted to elite universities just to provide a diversity of viewpoints that make for an interesting class discussion with other students and professors for four years; admissions also provides an opportunity to enjoy greater professional success for the following forty years—so fairness is important.

Moreover, if universities are truly concerned about diversity, attention to race alone is insufficient because it fails to provide more than a 10 percent representation to the bottom economic half. If diversity is defined broadly, to value differences in all kinds of circumstances—youths from trailer homes and ghettos and barrios as well as suburban minorities—economic affirmative action would add a great deal to the composition of elite colleges that race-based affirmative action alone does not provide.

The Supreme Court's majority opinion in *Grutter* does leave the door open for an eventual shift to economic affirmative action programs. The Court declares that universities must engage in "periodic reviews to determine whether racial preferences are necessary to achieve student body diversity." The opinion then points to universities in California, Florida, and Washington that are "engaged in experiments with a wide variety of alternative approaches."[23] Economic affirmative action is an important component of those experiments. The University of California uses "comprehensive review"—examining academic accomplishments in light of such obstacles as "low family income," "first generation to attend college," and "disadvantaged social or educational environment."[24] The University of Washington looks at academic achievement in the context of "family income, number in family, parents' educational level, [and] high school free lunch percent."[25] And the University of Florida's "Profile Assessment" program provides a leg up to "students who are poor, attend a low performing high school, or whose parents didn't attend college."[26]

Of course, the Supreme Court decision in *Grutter* will not end the debate over affirmative action but merely move it from the legal to the political sphere. Already, Ward Connerly, the author of successful anti–affirmative action initiatives in California and Washington, has vowed to take his fight to Michigan and elsewhere. This should give concern to supporters of affirmative action. Carnevale and Rose find that support for racial affirmative action in higher education is very thin, yet they find solid public support for consideration of economic obstacles. This finding comports with a wide body of public opinion research over several years.[27]

Three recent polls from January and February 2003 are illustrative. A *Los Angeles Times* survey found that, by 56–26 percent, Americans agreed with President Bush's opposition to the University of Michigan's racial preference plan. (Even Democrats narrowly supported Bush.) A *Newsweek* poll found Americans opposed preferences for blacks in university admissions by 68–26 percent. And an EPIC/MRA poll found Americans oppose the University of Michigan's affirmative action plan 63–27 percent. By contrast, Americans in these same polls supported preferences for low-income or economically disadvantaged students of all races by 65–28 percent (*Newsweek*), 59–31 percent (*Los Angeles Times*), and 57–36 percent (EPIC/MRA).[28] Many other countries pursue such economic affirmative action policies in place of racial affirmative action.[29]

What will happen to racial diversity if Connerly and colleagues are successful and universities turn to economic affirmative action as an alternative? At the top universities, Carnevale and Rose find that a race-blind economic affirmative action program would boost African American and Latino admissions from 4 percent (under a system strictly of grades and test scores) to 10 percent, down from the current 12 percent representation.[30]

Carnevale and Rose's economic affirmative action model does not sustain the present level of racial diversity in part because data show that even middle-class African Americans lag in achievement on average.[31] Blacks and Latinos are more likely to attend schools with a high incidence of poverty than whites of similar income—which imposes a disadvantage on minority students. These racial patterns reflect differing concentrations of neighborhood poverty, which are in turn a reflection of housing discrimination in large measure. One recent study found that black families with incomes in excess of $60,000 live in neighborhoods with higher poverty rates than white families earning less than $30,000.[32] Others have noted that middle-class blacks are generally newer arrivals to the middle-income status than whites and that even among whites and blacks of similar income, blacks command fewer financial assets. While black median income is 62 percent of white income, black median net worth is just 12 percent of white net worth.[33] Whereas income reflects a snapshot in time, wealth measures the accumulation of income (or debt) over generations and captures the legacy of slavery and segregation.[34]

But economic affirmative action could respond to both of these forms of discrimination indirectly. In defining obstacles, a university should consider not only the characteristics measured by Carnevale and Rose (parental income, education, and occupation and the high school's socioeconomic status) but also neighborhood affluence and net worth. Counting these additional family circumstances should boost racial diversity beyond the 10 percent figure that the more limited definition of economic disadvantage yields. At UCLA Law School, for example, under a program counting wealth and single-parent family status alongside more traditional socioeconomic concerns, in the fall 2002 entering class African Americans were 11.4 times as likely to be admitted as through other programs, and Latinos were 5.6 times as likely to be admitted.[35]

Carnevale and Rose's study does not provide support for the other major race-neutral alternative to racial affirmative action: the class rank approach, which is backed vigorously by the Bush administration. In three states, students are automatically admitted to public universities if they rank in the top echelon of their high school class, irrespective of standardized test scores or other qualifications. In California, a student must be in the top 4 percent; in Texas, the top 10 percent; and in Florida, the top 20 percent. How would these plans work at the nation's most selective 146 colleges?

The biggest problem is that if selective colleges were to ignore standardized tests completely, they would admit many students who are likely to drop out. Because high schools differ so widely in quality, graduation rates at the top 146 colleges, which now stand at 86 percent would plummet, Carnevale and Rose find.[36] African American and Hispanic students would be particularly likely to drop out, they conclude. Although preliminary experience with Texas has not shown increased dropout rates among students admitted under the class rank plan, this appears in some measure to reflect the fact that a relatively small percentage of eligible students take advantage of the program (about 700 of the state's 1,800 schools still do not send a single graduating senior to the flagship campus, the University of Texas at Austin).[37] It also is possible that the problems of inadequate preparation might be more glaring in the most competitive colleges.[38]

If one tried to remedy the dropout problem by using a class rank plan with a minimum level of readiness (say, 1000 on the SAT), graduation rates would remain high, but the proportion of blacks and Hispanics enrolled would drop, from 12 percent today to 7 percent under a top 10 percent class rank plan, and to 8 percent under a top 20 percent plan.

Other problems arise as well. On the grounds of "fairness," if admissions officers ought to look at merit in the context of obstacles overcome, the percentage plans ignore not only a critical component of achievement (standardized test scores) but also vital measures of obstacles overcome (consideration of parental income, education, occupation, and wealth). Those who go to the more embattled high schools are, on the whole, more likely to be disadvantaged themselves; but Carnevale and Rose's data suggest that economically better-off students disproportionately benefit from the class rank approach. Even in the poorest schools, nearly 60 percent of students in the top 10 percent of class rank come from the top two economic quartiles, they find. In short, the percentage plans would appear to be another dodge avoiding the root source of inequality: the division between the haves and have-nots.

CONCLUSION

In a sense, the debate over affirmative action at selective institutions reflects in miniature the larger debate about equity in higher education. Will we ever squarely face up to the fundamental inequalities rooted in economic class? The congressional reauthorization of the Higher Education Act and the ongoing debates in state capitals and within individual universities will help answer that enduring question. Low-income and working-class students of all colors constitute America's great untapped resource. The chapters in this volume provide important new data and ideas to help those students realize their full potential—for their sake and for ours.

1

LOW-INCOME STUDENTS AND THE AFFORDABILITY OF HIGHER EDUCATION

Lawrence E. Gladieux

Opportunities for college education remain sharply unequal in America. Students from families of low- and moderate-income backgrounds attend and graduate from college at much lower rates than those from the middle- and upper-income echelons.

This chapter examines these gaps in opportunity and the extent to which financial barriers may explain them. In so doing, it looks at trends in the affordability of higher education, pressures driving the tuition spiral, perceptions and the politics of the affordability issue, recent policy developments, and emerging challenges in ensuring access to postsecondary education for the incoming generation of students. It closes with a summary of recommendations for federal, state, and institutional policymakers.

Above all, it calls for a restoration of need-based principles for financing students in higher education, in the interest of equity as well as efficient allocation of public and private resources. In recent years the country has shifted attention, incentives, and revenues away from students and families with the greatest need. It is these students for whom financial assistance is likely to make a difference, expanding individual opportunity and boosting the country's net investment in higher education.

Progress but with Persistent Gaps

For most of the past half century, access to some form of postsecondary education or training has grown steadily for just about every group in our society. Sheer economic incentives have primarily driven this growth in postsecondary participation. Forces running deep in our economy have ratcheted up skill and credential requirements in the job market, putting a premium on education beyond high school.

There are no guarantees in life, with or without a college diploma, and the economic returns to investment in education can vary widely by type of degree and program. But the odds are increasingly stacked against those with the least education and training. As reflected in Figure 1.1, the more years of formal education one has, the more, on average, one earns. And, as illustrated in Figure 1.2, the earnings advantage of the most highly educated workers increased during the 1980s and 1990s. These trends have been absorbed into the conventional wisdom. People understand that the decision to attend college, and often which particular college and course of study, determines more than ever who has entrée to the best jobs and life chances.

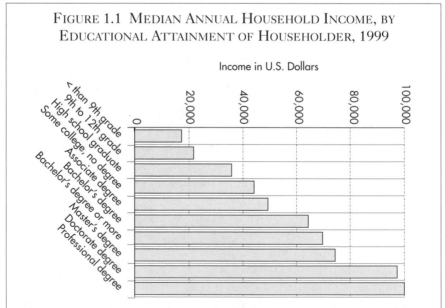

FIGURE 1.1 MEDIAN ANNUAL HOUSEHOLD INCOME, BY EDUCATIONAL ATTAINMENT OF HOUSEHOLDER, 1999

Source: U.S. Census Bureau, March Current Population Survey, Income Statistics Branch/HHES Division (Washington, D.C.: U.S. Department of Commerce, 2001), Table F-18.

FIGURE 1.2 INCOME BY EDUCATIONAL ATTAINMENT FOR PERSONS 18 YEARS OLD AND OVER, 1975–1999 (Inflation adjusted for 2001)

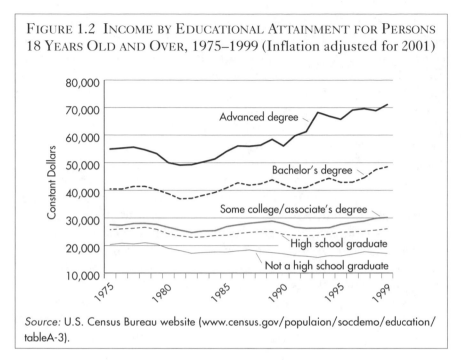

Source: U.S. Census Bureau website (www.census.gov/populaion/socdemo/education/tableA-3).

The good news is that more people are attaining higher levels of education and filling millions of skilled, high-paying jobs generated by a still strong economy. The bad news is that wage and wealth disparities have reached unprecedented extremes, and the least educated and skilled are getting a smaller and smaller piece of the pie. Education and training alone will not solve structural problems in the employment system that are tending to widen gaps between rich and poor. It is clear, however, that postsecondary education is more important than ever to the individual and to society.

WHO GOES TO COLLEGE?

More than fifty years ago the original GI Bill demonstrated to skeptics in both government and academia that higher education could and should serve a much wider segment of society. More than thirty-five years ago, during the Civil Rights movement and President Lyndon Johnson's War on Poverty, Congress passed the Higher Education Act and committed the federal government to the goal of opening college doors to all, regardless of family income or wealth.

Federal student aid has helped millions of people go to college. Federal, state, and private efforts combined have fueled a half century of explosive growth in college attendance and educational attainment. Degree-granting U.S. colleges and universities enrolled nearly 15 million students in 1998, two and a half times the number enrolled in 1965, more than six times the enrollment in 1950, and ten times pre–World War II levels.[1] Twenty-five percent of today's population over twenty-five years of age have completed four years of college or more, compared to 5 percent in 1940.[2]

In virtually every country of the world, participation in higher education—rates of entry and completion as well as type and prestige of institution attended—is closely associated with socioeconomic status. This association may be less pronounced in the United States, as we have created one of the most open, accessible postsecondary systems in the world. But the gaps in who benefits from higher education are persistent nonetheless.

Figure 1.3, based on census reports, traces a broad index of postsecondary participation for eighteen- to twenty-four-year-old high school graduates over the past three decades. All income groups show

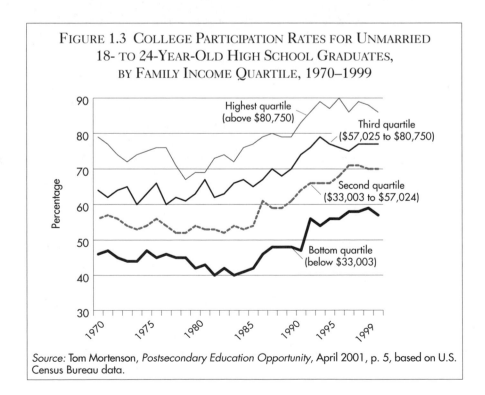

FIGURE 1.3 COLLEGE PARTICIPATION RATES FOR UNMARRIED
18- TO 24-YEAR-OLD HIGH SCHOOL GRADUATES,
BY FAMILY INCOME QUARTILE, 1970–1999

Source: Tom Mortenson, *Postsecondary Education Opportunity,* April 2001, p. 5, based on U.S. Census Bureau data.

gains. But low-income students attend college at much lower rates than high-income students, and participation gaps are about as wide if not wider today than they were in the early 1970s. In 1999, 86 percent of those in the top income quartile had experienced some postsecondary education, compared to 57 percent in the bottom quartile.

WHO GOES WHERE?

Where students go can be as important as whether they go. Students attending less than four-year schools reap lesser economic rewards on average than those who end up with a bachelor's degree or more. This is not at all to say that the bachelor's is the only measure of parity—far from it. "Going to college" means many things and produces many outcomes. Our society needs a range of subbaccalaureate opportunities, providing skills and credentials for survival in a complex economy. And our culture needs to confer more status and value on nonbaccalaureate education.[3]

Yet it is a reality that institutional choice is closely linked to a student's family background. Only one of five students from the bottom socioeconomic quartile enroll in a four-year institution within two years following high school graduation, compared to two of three from the top quartile.[4] Of college freshmen in fall 1999, one in six of the poorest attended a selective four-year college, while four in ten attended two-year community colleges. By comparison, one of two of the richest freshmen was enrolled in a selective four-year institution, and only one in ten attended a community college.[5]

WHO COMPLETES?

The most important question is whether students complete their programs—at whatever level—and receive their degree or certificate. Some students fall short of a degree and yet go on to productive careers, but the U.S. economy and labor market rely heavily on credentials.

Postsecondary participation has soared during the past quarter century, yet the proportion of college students completing degrees of any kind has remained flat. Given the growing diversity of students and the increasing complexity of their attendance patterns, stable completion rates may be a reasonable outcome. But the nation needs to do much better.

Roughly three-quarters of high school seniors go on to higher studies. Half receive some type of degree within five years of entering postsecondary education, and about one-quarter receive a bachelor's degree or higher. As shown in Figure 1.4, the most privileged students graduate at much higher rates than their less-advantaged counterparts: better than 40 percent of students in the top socioeconomic quartile graduate with a four-year degree, compared to only 6 percent of students in the lowest quartile. And white students are considerably more likely to receive a bachelor's degree than black and Hispanic students.

Students who go to college directly after high school and attend full time complete their programs in much higher proportions than other students. Delayed entry, part-time attendance, and other deviations from this traditional path result in lower persistence rates (the measure of progress toward graduation), and disadvantaged students are much more likely than not to take a nontraditional route. At the subbaccalaureate level these patterns are magnified. Associate's degree

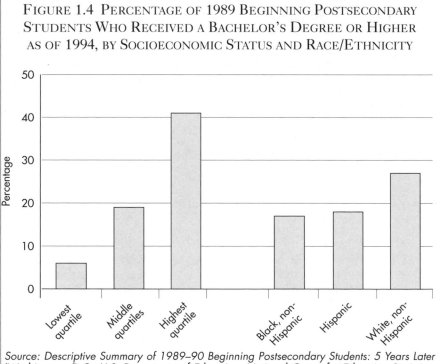

FIGURE 1.4 PERCENTAGE OF 1989 BEGINNING POSTSECONDARY STUDENTS WHO RECEIVED A BACHELOR'S DEGREE OR HIGHER AS OF 1994, BY SOCIOECONOMIC STATUS AND RACE/ETHNICITY

Source: Descriptive Summary of 1989–90 Beginning Postsecondary Students: 5 Years Later (Washington, D.C.: U.S. Department of Education, National Center for Education Statistics, 1996).

completion rates are in the 20–25 percent range, and these have changed little over the past twenty-five years.

As indicated in Figure 1.1, adults who have had "some college" earn more, on average, than those who stopped with a high school diploma. For both society and the individual the economic return on investment in many forms of postsecondary training has been on the rise. But while there may be a payoff to some college attendance, there is a considerably greater return to completion.

Getting students in the door is not good enough. Along with young people who do not finish high school and those who stop their education with a high school diploma, postsecondary non-degree earners fall into what has been called "the forgotten half" of our nation's youth and young adult population.[6] Some of these students may be left worse off if they have borrowed to finance their studies—as is increasingly the case for low-income students. They leave college with no degree, no skills, and a debt to repay.

WHY ARE THE GAPS SO WIDE?

National policy has focused for the better part of four decades on access to the system. But the greater challenge is to increase the likelihood that students actually succeed in reaching their goals, which in most cases means completing a degree.

Many circumstances influence an individual's chances of enrollment and success in higher education: prior schooling and academic achievement, the rigor and pattern of courses taken in secondary school, family and cultural attitudes, motivation and awareness of opportunities, campus environment and support—as well as ability to pay.[7] For low- and moderate-income students, affordability is intertwined with a host of other variables rooted in culture, environment, and societal expectations.

The problem of unequal opportunity has proved more intractable than anyone anticipated in the early years of the Higher Education Act. In the late 1960s and early 1970s, widely publicized reports showed that a college-age youth from a wealthy family was five times more likely to enroll in college than a youth from a poor family. The Carnegie Commission on Higher Education and other national groups called for federal leadership and need-based financial aid to equalize opportunities for college education.[8] As originally conceived, federal student aid was meant to send an early signal to young people and their families that college was a realistic goal. Sponsors of the Pell Grant in particular hoped that the promise of aid would have a powerful motivational effect.[9]

Today's student aid system seems to fall short of such visions. This is not to say that aid programs have failed, only that too much may have been expected of them. In their book *Beating the Odds: How the Poor Get to College*, Arthur Levine and Jana Nidiffer conclude that "financial aid is a necessary but insufficient condition" for equalizing college opportunities.[10]

The chapter in this volume written by Arthur M. Hauptman and P. Michael Timpane focuses on issues of academic preparation in expanding college opportunity for low-income students. Yet, these issues and those of a financial nature are intertwined, and both sets must be addressed in any strategy for improvement.

That not all the financial barriers to college have been removed is most plainly seen in data on participation rates by family income and academic preparation. An analysis by John Lee demonstrates that, at all levels of academic achievement, less affluent students attend college at rates considerably lower than more affluent students. Table 1.1 shows the percentage of 1992 high school graduates who had enrolled in postsecondary education by 1994, by socioeconomic status of the student's family and performance on a standardized achievement test. A student from the highest socioeconomic quartile and the lowest test score quartile was as likely to have enrolled in college as a student from the lowest socioeconomic quartile and the highest aptitude quartile. Put more informally, the least bright rich kids have as much chance of going to college as the smartest poor kids.

TRENDS IN AFFORDABILITY

Recent trends in tuition, family income, and financial aid policy have hit hardest students at the low end of the economic scale, those least able to afford postsecondary education. Figure 1.5 traces the growth of tuition—the published or "sticker" price of higher education—over the past three decades. (See Appendix A, page 54, for a definition of terms.) Adjusted for inflation, college prices were nearly flat in the

TABLE 1.1 PERCENTAGE OF 1992 HIGH SCHOOL GRADUATES ATTENDING COLLEGE IN 1994, BY SOCIOECONOMIC STATUS (SES) AND ACHIEVEMENT TEST QUARTILE

	Lowest Quartile SES	Middle Two Quartiles SES	Highest Quartile SES	Average
Lowest Quartile on Achievement Test	36	49	77	47
Second Quartile on Achievement Test	50	66	85	66
Third Quartile on Achievement Test	63	79	90	80
Highest Quartile on Achievement Test	78	89	97	93
Average	49	71	91	72

Source: John B. Lee, "How Do Students and Families Pay for College?" in Jacqueline E. King, ed., *Financing a College Education: How It Works, How It's Changing* (Phoenix, Ariz.: American Council on Education and Oryz Press, 1999), p. 15, based on U.S. Department of Education data.

FIGURE 1.5 AVERAGE TUITION AND FEES (ENROLLMENT-WEIGHTED), 1971–1972 TO 2001–2002, IN CONSTANT DOLLARS

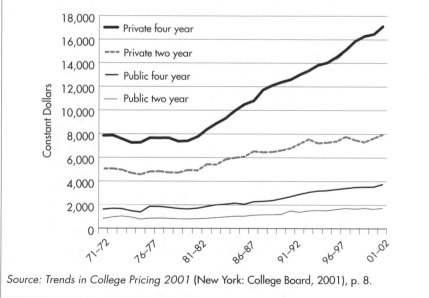

Source: Trends in College Pricing 2001 (New York: College Board, 2001), p. 8.

1970s, then began to soar after 1980. Tuition rose at twice and sometimes three times the consumer price index (CPI) in the 1980s and
1990s.

Figure 1.6 compares growth in tuition, family income, and student
aid from 1980 to 2000. Average, inflation-adjusted tuition more than
doubled at both public and private four-year institutions, while median family income rose only 27 percent. Student financial aid increased
in total value but not by enough to keep up with the rise in tuition.

Median family income tells only part of the story because incomes
have grown steadily less equitable during the past two decades. As
shown in Figure 1.7, the cost of attendance as a share of income has
increased for many families, but it has gone up the most for those
with less to begin. For a low-income family, the average annual bill for
attending a public four-year institution represented nearly 60 percent
of income in 2001–2002, up from 42 percent in 1971–72. For a middle-income family, the comparable figures were 16 percent of income
in 2001–2002 and 13 percent in 1971–72; for a high-income family, 5
percent of income in 2001–2002 and 6 percent in 1971–72.

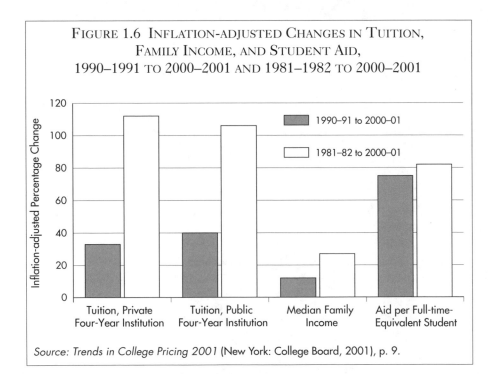

FIGURE 1.6 INFLATION-ADJUSTED CHANGES IN TUITION,
FAMILY INCOME, AND STUDENT AID,
1990–1991 TO 2000–2001 AND 1981–1982 TO 2000–2001

Source: *Trends in College Pricing 2001* (New York: College Board, 2001), p. 9.

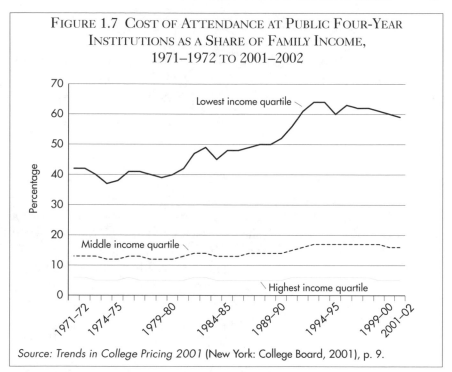

FIGURE 1.7 COST OF ATTENDANCE AT PUBLIC FOUR-YEAR
INSTITUTIONS AS A SHARE OF FAMILY INCOME,
1971–1972 TO 2001–2002

Source: Trends in College Pricing 2001 (New York: College Board, 2001), p. 9.

These estimates of burden reflect sticker prices, not the discounted prices that students and families might pay following award of student aid and other direct subsidies. There is evidence, however, that many low- and moderate-income students are unaware of available aid or are deterred by the rules, forms, and procedures required to obtain it.[11] Research suggests that lower-income students are more sensitive to tuition increases than middle- and upper-income students.[12] Thus, "sticker shock" appears to be at least as influential as net price (what students pay after aid prospects are considered) in determining whether and where less affluent students go to college.

Even after factoring in both student aid and the family's ability to pay as defined by standard need analysis (discussed later in this chapter), calculations of unmet need still suggest that the burden is greatest for low-income students. According to the Advisory Committee on Student Financial Assistance, unmet need is considerably higher for low-income students than for middle- and high-income students at both public and private four-year institutions as well as public two-year colleges.[13] Financial aid, in other words, has not offset the real increases in sticker price over the past two decades.

To fill the gap, students with unmet needs often must make extra-
ordinary efforts to stay in their programs, attending part time and intermittently, stretching out their education, living off campus, working
long hours, and going into debt. Yet, the probability of their persisting
and completing their degrees declines as a result of such patterns.[14]

GRANT-LOAN BALANCE

On top of these trends in tuition and ability to pay, the aid students
receive increasingly comes in the form of borrowing. Over the past
quarter century, student aid has drifted from a grant-based toward a
loan-based system. Figure 1.8 shows how the balance of loan and grant
aid has shifted over time. Twenty years ago, grants accounted for 55
percent and loans 41 percent of available aid (with work-study making
up the rest). Ten years ago the proportions of grant and loan aid were
about even. Today loans account for almost 60 percent of the total.

In 2000–2001 federally sponsored programs generated nearly
$39 billion in student and parent loans, five times the size of the Pell

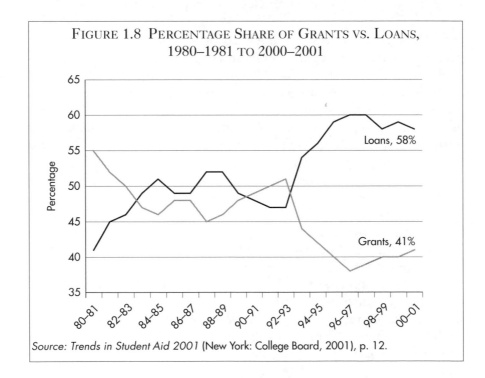

FIGURE 1.8 PERCENTAGE SHARE OF GRANTS VS. LOANS,
1980–1981 TO 2000–2001

Source: Trends in Student Aid 2001 (New York: College Board, 2001), p. 12.

Grant program that was meant to be the system's foundation, serving students with the greatest need.[15] As shown in Figure 1.9, since the late 1970s the maximum Pell Grant has dwindled relative to the price of higher education. Recent increases in Pell Grant appropriations have helped to stabilize the overall balance of aid in the system. Yet, the maximum Pell Grant, at $4,000 in 2002–2003, remains well below the purchasing power it had twenty-five years ago. Today's maximum covers about 40 percent of the average fixed costs (tuition and fees, room, and board) at a four-year public college and 15 percent at a private four-year college.

The Pell Grant was enacted in 1972 with much hope and idealism, and some observers have been disappointed with the results. As noted, wide gaps in opportunity persist. Yet, we do know that participation rates of low-income students have risen during the past quarter century. While behavioral research is inadequate to isolate the effects of student aid (much less a particular program) from all the other forces driving college enrollment, it seems unlikely that these gains would have been made without the existence of Pell Grants.

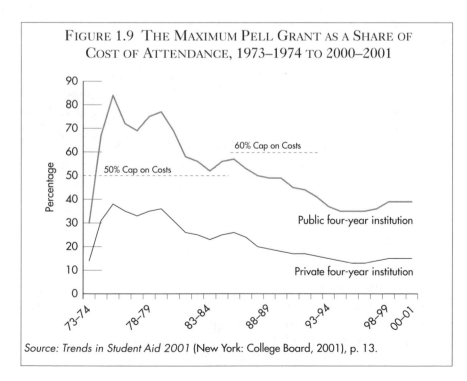

FIGURE 1.9 THE MAXIMUM PELL GRANT AS A SHARE OF COST OF ATTENDANCE, 1973–1974 TO 2000–2001

Source: *Trends in Student Aid 2001* (New York: College Board, 2001), p. 13.

The early promise shown by the program validates the case for significant expansion of the Pell Grant today. When the value of the maximum grant was at its peak in the middle and late 1970s, there were substantial increases in college-going rates for both men and women from poor backgrounds. At the same time states were expanding their grant programs for student aid, and colleges were making major efforts to recruit low-income, especially minority, students. But the new Pell Grant made a significant difference when added to the mix.[16]

Some skeptics worry whether higher education institutions simply substitute federal aid for what they would have provided themselves. Research suggests that institutions do alter their policies as a result of federal initiatives like Pell Grants, but for the most part the result is to free up resources for other deserving students. The availability of Pell Grant dollars has allowed some institutions to invest more of their own resources in students who are financially above the Pell Grant eligibility range but still of moderate means. Older, independent students may have reaped the largest benefit, in view of the large increases in their enrollment as a result of Pell Grants.[17]

The original Higher Education Act of 1965 called for need-based grants for the disadvantaged while helping middle-class families with government-guaranteed but minimally subsidized bank loans. Yet, today many students who were never expected to borrow when these programs were created are having to go into debt. Students most at risk—those who are underprivileged, those in remediation, students taking short-term training with uncertain returns—increasingly must take on the burden of loans for postsecondary education.

Among undergraduates, low-income students pursuing four-year degrees borrow the most. Of graduating seniors from low-income backgrounds in 1999, 80 percent in private four-year colleges and 65 percent in public four-year colleges had used loans to offset their college expenses. The proportion of high-income students who had borrowed was 57 percent in private four-year colleges and 47 percent in public four-year institutions. On average the low-income student accumulated more debt than the high-income student, especially at private institutions (see Table 1.2).

Effects of the shift to loan financing are difficult to ascertain, but the prospect of debt probably discourages many less affluent young people from considering postsecondary education. There is evidence as well that financial assistance in the form of loans is

TABLE 1.2
PERCENTAGE OF GRADUATING SENIORS WITH FEDERAL
STUDENT LOAN DEBT AND AVERAGE AMOUNT
BORROWED, BY FAMILY INCOME, 1999–2000

Family Income	PUBLIC FOUR-YEAR		PRIVATE FOUR-YEAR	
	Percentage Who Had Borrowed	Average Amount Borrowed	Percentage Who Had Borrowed	Average Amount Borrowed
Less than $30,000	65	$13,360	80	$17,270
$30,000–$49,999	55	$14,900	72	$16,775
$50,000–$69,999	58	$14,550	71	$16,285
$70,000 or more	47	$12,690	57	$15,250
Average	54	$13,680	66	$16,150

Source: U.S. Department of Education, National Postsecondary Student Aid Society, 1999–2000. Dependent students only.

less effective than grant aid in helping students to stay in college and get their degrees.[18] And there are consequences for society that must be considered as rising college costs are increasingly financed by student loans. The growth in debt may skew students' professional and career choices, discouraging college graduates from entering teaching and other socially useful fields that are relatively low paying.

ARE STUDENTS BORROWING TOO MUCH OR WORKING TOO MUCH?

The clearest generalization one can draw from survey research on how students finance their education is that it is difficult to generalize about what works best for different students. The broad majority of student borrowers assume manageable levels of debt and are making a sound investment in their future. Most will be able to repay, especially if they have received a degree or certificate. The federal student loan cohort default rate, which measures defaults in the first two years of repayment, has declined from 22 percent in 1990 to 6 percent in 2000.

Yet, policymakers continue to worry about the borrowing trend, and they should, for the several reasons already noted in this chapter. Some students get in over their heads, depending on their fields of study and income prospects in an uncertain economy. And student debt levels are rising, especially with the growing availability of private loans and commercial credit cards (See Box 1.1).

A more common financing strategy that students use is work, which can be at least as problematic as loans. One-third of all undergraduates (including those enrolled in four-year as well as two-year institutions) borrow in a given year; 80 percent of undergraduates work. Again, generalizations are hazardous, as individual circumstances vary widely. Yet, research by Jacqueline King suggests that many of these students work long hours, often to avoid borrowing, and doing so may not be in their best interest either academically or economically. For low-income students without sufficient grant aid, the financing choices are especially tough. Borrowing may be a pitfall, but working too much lengthens time to graduation and may jeopardize ultimately getting a degree.[20]

EROSION OF NEED-BASED STANDARDS

While students are borrowing as well as working more, the focus of federal policy has evolved from helping students who "but for such aid" would not be able to attend college, to relieving the burden for those who probably would go without such support. The antipoverty origins of the 1965 Higher Education Act have faded into history as eligibility for federal student aid has been extended up the economic ladder.

This development has been double-edged. On the one hand, the broadening of eligibility has popularized student financial aid with the middle class and thus strengthened the programs' political base. The Middle Income Student Assistance Act of 1978 probably helped to protect these programs politically from what could have been worse cutbacks in the early 1980s. On the other hand, the shift has diluted the federal emphasis on subsidies for low-income students and led to the predominance of loans in the mix of available aid.

BOX 1.1
TOWARD A LOAN-CENTERED AID SYSTEM

How did public higher education policy come to rely so heavily on student and parent borrowing to pay for college charges? The drift toward a loan-centered aid system dates back to the late 1970s, when Congress passed the Middle Income Student Assistance Act of 1978. That legislation modestly expanded eligibility for Pell Grants but, more significantly, made subsidized guaranteed loans available to any student regardless of income or need (the major subsidy to the borrower being government payment of interest during the student's period of enrollment). A year later Congress ensured banks a favorable rate of return on guaranteed student loans by tying subsidies to changes in Treasury bill rates. With the economy moving into a period of double-digit inflation and interest rates, student loan volume and associated federal costs skyrocketed. During the budgetary retrenchment of the early Reagan years, loan eligibility and subsidies were scaled back, but as an entitlement that had suddenly become popular with the middle class, guaranteed student loans proved the most resilient form of aid. Loan volume continued to grow, although more slowly than between 1978 and 1981.

When Congress reauthorized the student aid programs in 1986 and 1992, the borrowing trend was a major focus of concern. Congressional leaders said they wanted to restore a better balance between grants and loans, but the legislative outcome in both years continued the policy drift in the opposite direction. In 1992 the prospect of a post–cold war "peace dividend" had fueled hopes that Pell Grants might be turned into a mandated spending program with automatic annual increases for inflation. However, the peace dividend never materialized, leaving no room under existing balanced budget rules for such an expansion. After this failure, Congress followed a path of less resistance and lower cost by boosting the dollar ceilings in the existing loan programs. The 1992 reauthorization bill also established an unsubsidized loan option, not restricted by need, intended to make loans available to middle-income students who had been squeezed out of eligibility for the regular, subsidized loan program.

All told, the principal impact of the 1992 legislation, far from correcting the grant-loan imbalance, was to expand borrowing capacity for students and parents at all income levels, spurring a 70 percent increase in federal student loan volume in the three years after the law took effect. Since then the growth of federal loan volume has slowed, while privately sponsored student and parent borrowing has mushroomed.[19]

Continued on page 34

BOX 1.1 (CONTINUED)
TOWARD A LOAN-CENTERED AID SYSTEM

Even as Congress hammered out the 1992 reauthorization bill, presidential candidate Bill Clinton was on the campaign trail promising to overhaul the student aid system if he was elected. Part of his proposal aimed to neutralize the effect of loan debt on students' career decisions by offering flexible repayment rates geared to borrowers' future income. A year later, in fact, President Clinton won congressional passage of the Student Loan Reform Act of 1993, altering the way student loans are financed, originated, and repaid. Among other things, the act included a plan that calibrated monthly repayment to a percentage of the borrower's income for up to twenty-five years. Relatively few students, however, have chosen this plan since it was implemented. Most borrowers continue to repay in fixed installments over ten years.

Changes brought about by the 1992 reauthorization of the Higher Education Act yielded another expansion in middle-income eligibility but with no corresponding increase in actual funds. The result has been to spread available aid more thinly, shifting scarce aid dollars up the income scale, at the expense of less well-off students.

The movement of federal policy away from need-based principles is reflected most dramatically in the $40 billion (estimated) of tuition tax breaks enacted as part of the Taxpayer Relief Act of 1997. The so-called Hope Scholarships[21] and Lifetime Learning Tax Credits primarily benefit middle- and upper-middle-income taxpayers who incur tuition expenses for postsecondary education. Along with Education IRAs and related provisions of the federal tax code, these benefits are projected to cost the U.S. Treasury more than $60 billion dollars in lost revenue over the next five years, 2003–2007. (See Appendix B for details.)

Likewise, many state governments are legislating tuition tax credits and deductions and are investing more heavily in non-need-based merit scholarships as well as college savings and prepaid plans oriented to middle- and upper-income families. And the colleges themselves have increasingly turned to merit-based aid and preferential packaging not necessarily based on need. (This chapter will return later to an exploration of state and institutional policy developments in greater depth.)

PERCEPTIONS AND POLITICS

For less affluent students, the adverse trends in affordability may be compounded by widespread misapprehensions about the expensiveness of a college education. Survey research by the American Council on Education indicates that most students and families significantly overestimate the average tuition charged by every type of institution: community college, public university, private liberal arts college, and private university. At the same time, they underestimate the availability of financial aid—again, by a wide margin.[22] The tuition spiral is real, but perceived barriers can be as effective as real ones. Such misapprehensions likely deter some Americans from pursuing a postsecondary education or enrolling in the school or program of their choice.

The media have contributed to the overreaction by their tendency to focus coverage on the most expensive institutions in the country. Journalists aim to produce good copy, and reporting on college prices going through the roof usually makes a better story than the complex reality of diverse prices and subsidies that characterize higher education finance. The media's intensity seemed to peak in 1996, when rising tuition made the cover of just about every major newsmagazine. The most sensational (and misleading) was *Newsweek*: "$1000 a Week: The Scary Cost of College." The article did not point out that less than 1 percent of students in the country faced such prices, and most such students received financial aid.

At the same time, polling and focus group research told politicians that paying for college was nearing the top of voters' concerns. Both national party platforms put a spotlight on college costs in 1996, and President Clinton effectively captured the theme in his reelection campaign, making it a centerpiece of his education agenda and his proposed middle-class tax cut. Governors, legislators, and political candidates of both parties have clamored to address the issue ever since.

Steadily rising college tuition and the accompanying drumbeat of the media and political campaigns have created public alarm and anxiety. In the policy arena, college affordability is increasingly cited as an issue that preoccupies middle- and upper-middle-income students and families. And it is to those groups that new incentives and subsidies are primarily being directed—those most likely to attend and to have the capacity to finance a college education in the first place. The generalized sense of crisis about paying for college has diverted attention and assistance away from those with the least ability to afford it.

WHAT IS DRIVING THE TUITION SPIRAL?

Exaggeration and overreaction aside, college costs continue to rise considerably faster than the CPI, and there is no consensus among policymakers and analysts as to why or how to curb the spiral. For one thing, the dynamics of setting tuition in the public and private sectors of higher education are substantially different. For public higher education, tuition is politically negotiated among institutions, state boards, legislators, governors, and other public officials. During the recession of the early 1990s many states hiked tuition sharply to make up for budget shortfalls. Political reaction to those increases along with economic recovery produced more moderate (but still above inflation) increases in the mid- and late-1990s in most states. The recent economic slowdown has started the cycle over again, putting renewed upward pressure on public college tuition as state revenues decline.

At independent institutions, tuition is more a function of "what the market will bear." Private college tuition rose most sharply in the 1980s, when these institutions invested heavily in faculty salaries and other needs, trying to recover ground lost to inflation in the 1970s. Private institutions also discovered in the 1980s that large tuition increases did not deter students and their families; in fact, escalating prices seemed to be viewed by many as an index of quality. But eventually a combination of bad publicity and fear of pricing themselves out of the market brought the private colleges back to more moderate rates of increase (though, again, still well ahead of inflation) in the 1990s.

In 1997 Congress established a National Commission on the Cost of Higher Education, which issued a report less than a year later saying there was no single, tidy explanation for the tuition spiral. The commission examined what sorts of pressures may be driving up institutional budgets and the underlying costs of providing instruction—everything from faculty salaries and facilities to technology, curriculum, government regulation, and expectations of students (and parents) about quality and amenities on campus. It concluded that "the available data on higher education expenditures and revenues make it difficult to ascertain direct relationships among the cost drivers and increases in the price of higher education. Institutions of higher education, even to most people in the academy, are financially opaque."[23]

The commission found some evidence that institutional financial aid is one of the cost and price drivers, concluding that tuition might have increased slightly less if institutions had not plowed so much revenue into such assistance packages. But the commission noted that if colleges had not invested in aid, students would have had to borrow more or access would have diminished. It dismissed any notion that the availability of federal grant aid might be a source of tuition increases. Less than one student in four receives a grant, which pays for only a portion of total cost of attendance in both the public and private sector. The commission was less conclusive about whether the broader availability of federal student loans might bear some relationship to rising costs and prices.

A part of the equation that the commission did not speak to directly was demand for the service. In some measure colleges and universities charge what they do because they can. No nonprofit institution sets tuition to recover the full costs of instruction, but many colleges could no doubt charge considerably higher tuition than they already do and still fill their classes (in some cases several times over). This is true of prestigious private institutions, which surely underprice their services in the pure economic sense of supply and demand. The same holds for flagship public institutions.

If the commission came short of pinpointing causes of the tuition spiral, the hottest political question before it was whether the federal government should try to contain college costs and prices. This was an especially sensitive issue at the time because Congress was about to review and reauthorize the Higher Education Act in 1998, and college leaders were worried that if the commission recommended some kind of cost controls, it might lead to a contentious debate in Congress and scrutiny of the financial practices of institutions, if not intrusive federal regulation.

In the end the commission said it was up to institutions to contain costs and do a better job of explaining their finances to students and families. It admonished the colleges to intensify their efforts to increase institutional productivity and to organize an awareness campaign to inform the public about the actual costs associated with postsecondary education, the prospective returns on investment in schooling, and preparation for college. As for the federal role, the commission called on the government to do a better job of collecting and reporting standardized data on costs, prices, and subsidies in higher education and of analyzing the relationship between tuition and institutional expenditures—but *not* to try to impose cost or price controls.

The essentially status quo outcome of the 1998 national commission study was neither surprising nor unreasonable. It is far from clear that the federal government has sufficient mandate (including constitutional authority) or political leverage to intervene constructively in tuition pricing by public or independent non-profit institutions of higher education. While the federal government contributes the lion's share of direct student aid, overall it provides less than 15 percent of revenues of colleges and universities. Members of Congress and other policymakers are understandably concerned with the tuition trend and will continue investigating and airing the issues on behalf of an anxious public. But in the final analysis federal officials are too far from the action and ought to leave cost containment and price setting to state and local authorities and market forces.

FEDERAL POLICY CHOICES

Also to no one's surprise, the national study commission called on Congress to continue the existing federal grant, loan, and work-study aid programs, to provide additional funding for them, and to simplify the delivery of student assistance. Historically, the federal government has exerted enormous leadership in trying to level the playing field in American higher education, from the Morrill Land Grant Act to the GI Bill and the Higher Education Act. Today federal programs generate nearly three-fourths of all aid available to help students and families pay the tuition, living costs, and related expenses of post-secondary education. (See Figure 1.10 for the principal sources and amounts of financial aid available to students in 2000–2001.)

With the enactment of the Taxpayer Relief Act of 1997, however, the federal government now has two ways of delivering college financial assistance: one through the tax code and one through ordinary spending programs. These two sets of benefits operate on different principles and serve different, though overlapping, populations. In general, under the tax code, the more income one has (up to the income ceilings established in the law), the more one benefits from particular tax provisions. Under the need-based student aid programs authorized by Title IV of the Higher Education Act, the less income one has, the more one benefits. In general, the tuition tax breaks go primarily to students and families with incomes above the median, while most Title IV assistance goes to families below the median.

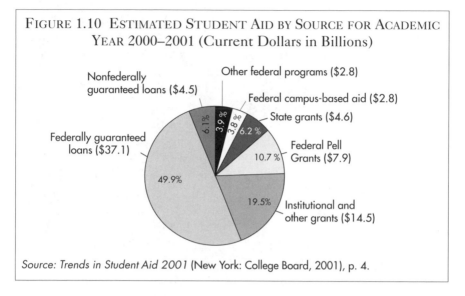

FIGURE 1.10 ESTIMATED STUDENT AID BY SOURCE FOR ACADEMIC
YEAR 2000–2001 (Current Dollars in Billions)

Nonfederally guaranteed loans ($4.5)

Other federal programs ($2.8)

Federal campus-based aid ($2.8)

State grants ($4.6)

Federally guaranteed loans ($37.1)

6.1% 3.9% 3.8% 6.2%

Federal Pell Grants ($7.9)

10.7%

49.9%

19.5%

Institutional and other grants ($14.5)

Source: *Trends in Student Aid 2001* (New York: College Board, 2001), p. 4.

Over the long haul, how will these two sets of benefits interact? Which will predominate? How will the federal government deliver the bulk of its assistance to students and families for managing post-secondary costs—through the tax code or through Title IV of the Higher Education Act? While this will not be a zero-sum game, these parallel systems will inevitably compete for resources over time.

While recent funding increases for Pell Grants have restored some of the buying power lost in this program since the 1970s, need-based grant support for students is still in a catch-up situation. Like other discretionary (nonentitlement) programs in the federal budget, Pell Grants have no guaranteed financing from year to year. By contrast, tuition tax breaks function, in effect, as an entitlement not tied to annual appropriations, and history suggests that once such benefits are written into the tax code, there will be persistent pressure over time to expand eligibility for them.

The Clinton administration argued consistently that the country needs to invest more in education and training to boost economic growth, expand opportunity, and reduce income disparities. But tuition tax breaks are not an effective means to achieve these worthy objectives. Above all, they are not a sound strategy for increasing access to education.

As one would expect, the Bush administration has not been a cheer-leader for such a signature Clinton legacy as the Hope Scholarships and

Lifetime Learning Tax Credits. But neither has the current administration proposed to eliminate or scale them back. In fact, when President Bush pushed his general tax cut through Congress in 2001, two amendments expanding tuition tax relief were included in the final legislation. One provided a deduction for tuition expenses incurred by relatively high-income families (namely, those with incomes up to $130,000; $160,000 starting in 2004), which exceeds the eligibility ceiling of $100,000 for Hope Scholarships and Lifetime Learning Tax Credits). The second amendment expanded the amount taxpayers can invest in an Education IRA, from $500 to $2,000 a year, and made the proceeds payable for K–12 schooling as well as postsecondary expenses.

As for Pell Grants, the Bush administration has supported annual increases but not as much as Congress has ultimately appropriated in the past two years. Partisan sparring over Pell Grant funding will no doubt intensify in the period ahead for two reasons. Deficits are projected to grow, putting a squeeze on all domestic discretionary spending in the federal budget. And the Pell Grant program itself has developed a shortfall; that is, Pell Grant payments have overrun the available appropriation in recent years, and no one has a ready solution for making up this shortfall while continuing to meet obligations.

During President Bush's election campaign in 2000, he advocated "front-loading" Pell Grants, meaning that first- and possibly second-year undergraduates would receive larger awards than upper-class students. The objective would be to boost access by using more of the Pell money to get disadvantaged students started in some kind of postsecondary education or training. The administration has yet to formalize this proposal, but the time to do so will be during the 108th Congress in (2003–2004), when the Higher Education Act is scheduled for reauthorization.

Front-loading Pell Grants would no doubt boost prospects for many students in community colleges and short-term training programs. But for students pursuing baccalaureate degrees, there is a bait-and-switch aspect to front-loading; as a result, it may not be conducive to completion of a degree program. There also are operational complexities that would have to be worked out, such as determining and verifying which students are in their first year.

Another idea from the Bush election campaign that has yet to be formalized is to provide matching grants to states to boost their sponsorship of merit scholarships. However, such federal incentives would be redundant. Most of the states have already created and are rapidly expanding merit scholarship programs, and federal outlays for this purpose would contribute little to solving the problem of access for low- and moderate-income students. Federal resources would be better directed to Pell Grants and other need-tested aid under Title IV of the Higher Education Act.

Bush administration officials say they are working on proposals for the next higher education reauthorization, but at this writing they have yet to release their plan. As with the administration's "No Child Left Behind" legislation for reform of K–12 schooling, these officials say, the primary goal will be to strengthen mechanisms for ensuring accountability and high performance of educational institutions participating in federal programs.

Whatever the administration might propose, the most consequential issue in the coming reauthorization cycle is likely to be whether and how much to raise student borrowing limits and what fees and interest rates borrowers should pay on their federally sponsored student loans. For budgetary reasons and because legislators did not want to fuel student indebtedness, Congress kept the lid on borrowing capacity in the 1998 reauthorization. This time around, at least modest increases seem inevitable, and one compelling reason will be to stem the growing dependence of students on private credit programs, which are invariably marketed at higher costs to the borrower than federally sponsored loans.

STATE STRATEGIES

A report by the National Center for Public Policy and Higher Education spotlights the wide range of strategies that the fifty states have adopted for increasing access to higher education.[24] Historically, all the states have relied in varying measure on free or low-tuition public higher education, providing general subsidies for all enrolled students. In recent decades, all of the states have invested to some degree as well in financial aid, providing more targeted student subsidies based on need and other criteria. Today each state relies on a different mix of policies—reflecting regional values, customs, and budgetary conditions—to make postsecondary opportunities affordable.

Overall, however, higher education's share of state revenues has gradually diminished since the late 1970s, and the proportion of public higher education costs financed by tuition has been increasing on average among the states—from 13 percent in 1981 to 19 percent in 1997.[25] Thus, students and families bear more of the burden than they did twenty years ago, which means that need-based financial aid has an increasingly important role in sustaining equal access to public colleges.

Some analysts of higher education finance have long advocated substantially increased public college tuition as a matter of policy, accompanied by greatly expanded financial assistance based on need. Instead of charging the same amount across the board, they urge more targeted subsidies, with wealthier students and their families contributing more than those with less ability to pay.[26] Few state policymakers embrace such a "high tuition/high aid" philosophy, but to the extent that public sector tuition continues to drift upward over time—for whatever reason—need-based aid becomes more critical.

Starting from a small base, state support for undergraduate grant programs has increased fourfold in real dollar terms since 1970, according to research by Donald Heller. These programs now provide more than $4 billion in financial aid annually. Heller reports that when they were first developed, most "mirrored the goal of the federal Title IV programs in the Higher Education Act of 1965, that of providing financial assistance to needy students."[27] The states may have used various criteria to determine academic qualifications, but the great majority of the programs took financial need into account.

A turning point, according to Heller, came in 1993, when Governor Zell Miller created the Georgia HOPE (Helping Outstanding Pupils Educationally) Scholarship Program, touching off a proliferation of state merit-based programs across the country. Since then, support for merit scholarships has boomed, while need-based aid has grown much more slowly. More than three-quarters of undergraduate grant awards made by the states are still based at least in part on financial need, but there has been a sharp turn in policy in the direction of rewarding academic ability and achievement. Such programs, Heller says, "use no means testing whatsoever; the children of the rich are as eligible for the scholarships as are the children of the poor."[28] They disproportionately help those who can afford college without such assistance and would likely attend in any case.

Meanwhile, nearly all fifty states have created so-called 529 plans that encourage parents to prepay the costs of their children's college education or set money aside in an investment fund dedicated to meet such future expenses.[29] Earnings and disbursements from these plans (dubbed "529" for the section of the Internal Revenue Code that defines "qualified state tuition programs") are now largely exempt from federal and state taxes. Some states also offer a tax deduction for the initial investment. Stimulating family savings for college is a good cause, and the college savings movement is booming with the development of the state-sponsored as well as commercial plans. But they benefit only those families who have sufficient discretionary income to put money aside for the future and sufficient taxable income to benefit from the related tax breaks. Subsidies for savings are not much help to those who can barely make ends meet.

Bucking the trend favoring cost relief for those who do not necessarily need it, California is one state that has recently tried to break new ground in extending access to higher education. In 2000 it enacted legislation converting the Cal Grant, the state's need-based grant program, into an entitlement. The law guarantees Cal Grants for every graduating high school applicant and every transferring community college student who meets the program's financial and academic requirements. The state has made a huge commitment to the coming generation of students, ensuring help for those who need it most. It has had difficulty bringing the new Cal Grant to full potential in its inaugural two years. But California, one hopes, can become a bellwether and model for other states and the nation in shoring up the principle of need-based aid while creating incentives for academic achievement.

INSTITUTIONAL AID

Colleges and universities supply more than $13 billion in aid to students, over and above federal and state sources. How do institutions invest these dollars?

The concept and practice of need analysis as the basis for awarding student financial aid was forged in the education community. A group of private colleges banded together in the 1950s in an effort to control their own tendencies to use financial aid for competitive advantage in the market for students. If they could agree on a common formula for targeting aid, the colleges figured, they could allocate available dollars more efficiently and equitably, allowing students to choose among institutions without price being a major consideration. In 1954 the colleges formed the College Scholarship Service

(CSS) as part of the College Entrance Examination Board ("College Board" for short). They resolved to follow consistent guidelines in measuring the financial need of aid applicants, replacing various rules of thumb previously used on campuses.

CSS in turn developed and distributed the Parents' Confidential Statement, a form for collecting common information on family finances, and by the late 1950s it was using electronic data processing to streamline the computation of estimated need. Need was calculated as the difference between total estimated student expenses (including books and transportation as well as tuition, room, and board) and the family's estimated ability to pay, or "expected family contribution."

Today a "federal methodology" of need analysis is embedded in the Higher Education Act to govern the award of federal aid. (Congress wrote this into the law in 1986 and 1992.) Many colleges use the federal methodology for awarding their own aid funds, whereas others use an "institutional methodology" maintained by the College Board, and an increasing number appear to be freelancing with their own variations of need analysis. The consensus that came out of the 1950s has unraveled in practice, and colleges are following their own compass in responding to competitive pressures.

Various forces have contributed to the erosion of need-based policies over the past decade. The legislation of a federal methodology essentially froze ability-to-pay rules into law. Rather than an evolving set of standards examined and adjusted from year to year by economists and experts in the education community, federal need analysis has become nearly static, prompting institutions to adopt divergent standards for awarding their own aid.

In the early 1990s the Justice Department conducted an antitrust investigation of the so-called Overlap Group, thirty or so elite and expensive private colleges that collectively considered aid applications and determined how much aid should be awarded in individual cases. While the purported aim of the investigation was to protect the right of consumers (students and their families) to get the best financial aid deal they could from the institutions, in truth the Justice Department acted on the basis of a rigid marketplace ideology that was not in the best interests of poor students. The Overlap Group was a cooperative arrangement much in the spirit of the 1950s agreement, with the objective of concentrating aid on those with the greatest need. On balance, its deliberations helped make the best use of scarce resources to keep these highly priced colleges open to low- and moderate-income students. The result of the antitrust action undermined sound social policy, with repercussions that were felt far beyond the Overlap Group. It was a catalyst in the splintering of need-based standards in the higher education community at large. Market forces were coming into play on their own, but the Justice Department action constrained any organized effort to mitigate their deleterious effects.

These market forces have been relentless, especially in the world of selective admissions, where low-income students may be increasingly disadvantaged by "need-sensitive" (taking ability to pay into account) and early decision policies. Many elite institutions now lock in from 30 to 50 percent of their incoming freshman class based on early admissions, and more and more students seem to be willing to make binding commitments early in their senior year of high school. But most of these are wealthy enough not to have to worry about financial aid. The early decision trend is not fair to poor students, who need to wait till the spring, when aid packages are decided.

In their book *The Student Aid Game*, Michael McPherson and Morton Schapiro detail the multiple ways that colleges are diverging from ability-to-pay principles and "leveraging" financial aid to maximize net tuition revenue and meet their "enrollment management" objectives.[30] McPherson and Schapiro's research, along with more recent analysis by Donald Heller,[31] documents the rapid growth of spending on merit scholarships and other non-need-based aid at a wide range of institutions, the shift in ostensibly need-based awards up the income scale, and the increasing proportion of institutional aid overall that has been awarded to more affluent students as a consequence.

Reversing these trends will not be easy. Market pressures are intense for most colleges. Competitive price discounting through student aid has become standard operating procedure. And the antitrust settlement of the early 1990s leaves a lingering question of legality regarding collective action within the higher education community to refocus aid policies on those with the greatest need.

THE COMING TIDAL WAVE OF STUDENTS

Figure 1.11 (page 46) traces live births in the United States since 1946. The post–World War II baby boom produced an explosion of college enrollments in the 1960s and 1970s. Now come the children of the

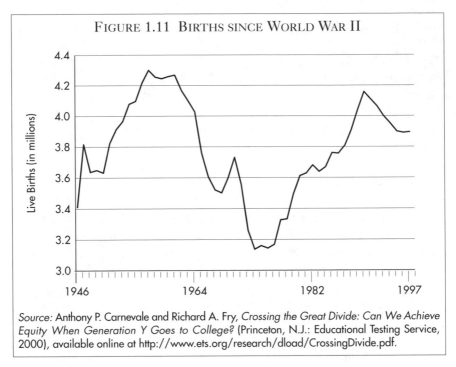

FIGURE 1.11 BIRTHS SINCE WORLD WAR II

Source: Anthony P. Carnevale and Richard A. Fry, *Crossing the Great Divide: Can We Achieve Equity When Generation Y Goes to College?* (Princeton, N.J.: Educational Testing Service, 2000), available online at http://www.ets.org/research/dload/CrossingDivide.pdf.

baby boomers, a cohort that will yield a somewhat smaller but still impressive expansion in the college-age population over the next fifteen years.

The Census Bureau projects that there will be five million more eighteen- to twenty-four-year-olds in the year 2010 than there were in 1995, an increase of more than 20 percent. The country is already experiencing the leading edge of this expansion in the pool of prospective high school graduates and college students. By one estimate there will be 2.6 million more undergraduates on campus in 2015 than there are today, a product of the baby-boom echo, rising immigration, and more adult learners.[32]

This cohort, however, will look considerably different from previous generations of college-age students. It will be more ethnically diverse, and the fastest growth will come from groups in our society that have traditionally been poorer than the general population and more educationally at risk.[33]

To increase—or even just to sustain—current levels of college participation is going to require aggressive policies, both to strengthen the readiness of students to undertake college-level work and to give low- and moderate-income students the financial assistance they need to pay for higher education. Even if college tuition charges grow no more rapidly than family incomes over the next fifteen years, the new demography of college-age students will require much greater financial aid to preserve postsecondary access and grant such students the chance for success.

RECOMMENDATIONS

To rise to this challenge means summoning a renewed spirit of partnership among the federal government, the states, and the colleges in expanding opportunity and meeting the country's need for a skilled and competitive workforce.

THE FEDERAL GOVERNMENT

Federal financial aid—aid that is generally targeted to students with the fewest resources and delivered to students and families as simply and predictably as possible—remains as important as when the Higher Education Act was passed in 1965. Today the federal government should give priority to the following policies:

KEEP THE FOCUS ON HELPING THOSE WITH THE GREATEST NEED. Historically, the federal government has exerted enormous leadership in this area, providing incentives to states and institutions to increase their investment in securing access and opportunity for lower-income students. But as has just been seen, recent policy shifts—the enactment of tuition tax breaks, the Justice Department's antitrust challenge to need-based aid agreements—have diluted the beneficial influence. In fact, the whole student aid system seems to be tilting toward cost relief for the middle and upper-middle class. The federal government should reassert its leadership in fostering need-based aid.

PUBLICIZE THE AID PROGRAMS AND MAKE THEM ACCESSIBLE TO THOSE WHO NEED HELP THE MOST. Middle-class families tend to be better informed and more aggressive in using the system, while lower-income families not only overestimate the price of college but often do not know how much help is available and how to get it. Information and outreach are especially important where high school guidance resources are inadequate. The Department of Education should more actively publicize available financial aid and procedures for attaining it through the TRIO, GEAR-UP (Gaining Early Awareness and Readiness for Undergraduate Programs), and community-based outreach programs, churches, schools, youth and adult learning centers, as well as the news media.

RESTORE THE PURCHASING POWER OF PELL GRANTS. This is the most straightforward action the federal government could take to help low-income students. The constant-dollar value of Pell Grant assistance was at its peak in the middle to late 1970s. Based on changes in the cost of attending college since then, restoring the purchasing power of the Pell program would require a maximum grant of more than $8,000, double the current maximum, which in turn would require a $12–15 billion boost in annual appropriations. As it happens, this is roughly the average annual amount of revenue that is projected to be lost to the Treasury from 2003 through 2007 as a result of the Hope Scholarships and Lifetime Learning Tax Credits, college savings incentives, and related tuition tax benefits that have been enacted since 1997. (See Appendix B for details.)

Such a major expansion of Pell Grants is far outside the incrementalist frame of reference of current budget discussions.[34] But this is what it would take to make the Pell Grant the powerful building block for low-income students it was intended to be. It should be noted that the more dollars invested in the program, the more help it is able to offer as well to moderate-income students who are now just out of range of Pell Grant eligibility.

MAKE THE PELL GRANT AN ENTITLEMENT PROGRAM. Tuition benefits written into the tax code tacitly amount to a new entitlement for middle- and upper-middle-income citizens. Pell Grants compete with other programs for annual appropriations, and real increases will not come easily under prevailing fiscal constraints. Neither will the idea of creating a substantial new entitlement program in the federal budget. But in fairness, and in anticipation of the coming tidal wave of students, a Pell Grant entitlement is much needed.

PROMOTE STUDENT SUCCESS, NOT JUST ACCESS. Access has been the touchstone of federal student aid policy for the past three decades. Future efforts should identify strategies that not only facilitate entry into the system but also give students a better chance to complete their programs, especially students who are financially and academically at risk. One approach would be for the federal government to provide financial incentives to institutions that enroll, assist, and graduate low-income students. A complementary approach would be regulatory: make effective academic support services a condition of institutional participation in the federal aid programs authorized by Title IV of the Higher Education Act.[35]

PROVIDE AN ANTITRUST EXEMPTION FOR COLLEGES TO AGREE ON NEED-BASED POLICIES. Current law allows colleges that maintain strictly need-blind admissions policies to confer and agree among themselves on assessment of need without danger of antitrust violation. This exemption should be widened to give colleges an open field for drawing up agreements that will help focus scarce aid dollars on students who actually need them in order to attend the institution of their choice.

ENCOURAGE RESPONSIBLE STUDENT BORROWING AND EASE REPAYMENT BURDENS. As the principal sponsor of student loans, the federal government should build coalitions of schools, colleges, lenders, loan guarantors, and state agencies to curb unnecessary borrowing and help students manage debt. Students need help in evaluating how much they should borrow based on their career interests and anticipated ability to repay.[36] Borrowers need to be reminded that there are flexible repayment options, including extended, graduated, and income-contingent repayment plans.

HELP POOR FAMILIES ESTABLISH NEST-EGG SAVINGS FOR THEIR CHILDREN'S EDUCATION. When Congress debated the Taxpayer Relief Act in 1997, some legislators were concerned that Education IRAs and other college savings incentives would only benefit middle- and upper-middle-income taxpayers. These legislators explored ways to balance the bill, like matching deposits or issuing refundable tax credits that might give effective incentives to the poor. No such solution made it into the final legislation, but the fairness issue has not gone away. The college savings industry is booming. Federal and state tax breaks for college savings are now substantial. Savings are critically important to making people feel that they have a stake in our society and economy—and in their own future. But not everyone has money to set aside or sufficient taxable income to benefit from tax subsidies. Lack of assets, not just lack of income, perpetuates the cycle of poverty and unequal opportunity.

Some policy analysts have argued for the establishment of "individual development accounts" (IDAs) for families below the poverty line. Each dollar a participant saves would be matched, provided that the proceeds are withdrawn only to pay for postsecondary education, to buy a home, or to start a business. In 1998 Congress funded a five-year IDA experiment, the results of which are being evaluated, and the Brookings Institution has published a book on asset-building strategies for the poor by Michele Miller-Adams, *Owning Up: Poverty, Assets, and the American Dream.*[37]

THE STATES

States have widely divergent policies on tuition pricing (for public institutions) and financial aid (for students in both public and private institutions). Whether they lean toward low tuition across the board or "high-tuition/high aid," states bear primary responsibility for ensuring broad access to higher education. Two obligations in particular rest with state governments:

EMPHASIZE NEED-BASED AID OVER MERIT SCHOLARSHIPS AND TAX-FAVORED TUITION FINANCING. The best and the brightest students have long been sought after by colleges and handsomely rewarded with subsidies, direct and indirect. And they always will be. State merit-based scholarships do not by and large expand access. Neither do state tuition tax incentives.

KEEP NEED-BASED STUDENT FINANCIAL AID IN STEP WITH TUITION INCREASES. Too often tuition and fees at public institutions end up as a filler or balancer in the state budget process, and too often student financial aid is an afterthought. Policymakers need to look at these decisions together in a way that relates them to state policy goals. Leaving aside theoretical arguments about full-cost pricing versus subsidized rates, the fact is that tuition is going up faster than the consumer price index and family income in most states. If student aid does not keep pace, college opportunity for less affluent students will surely suffer.

The Colleges

Individual colleges caught up in a supercharged competition for survival or academic prestige may not feel they have many degrees of freedom in today's market. Yet their actions and policies are critical to promoting broad access to higher education. Institutions of higher learning should heed these imperatives:

DO A BETTER JOB OF CONTAINING COSTS AND PRICES AND EXPLAINING THEM TO A SKEPTICAL PUBLIC. Students and families do not believe that colleges are doing enough to curb the tuition spiral. The National Commission on the Cost of Higher Education said the federal government should stay out of these matters, and it should, but colleges need to make their finances more transparent.

HELP STUDENTS UNDERSTAND THE RISKS AND BENEFITS OF THEIR FINANCING OPTIONS. Some students arrive on campus without the necessary financial literacy or maturity to make sound choices about borrowing, credit cards, work, or housing, to say nothing of academic course loads and selections. Colleges should make a greater effort to link academic advising and counseling on money matters, helping students to choose financing strategies that support their academic goals.[38]

HALT THE TREND TOWARD NEED-SENSITIVE AND EARLY ADMISSIONS. Low- and moderate-income students are primarily concerned with financial aid and are not as free to play the early decision game as wealthier students. College admissions should be a level playing field regardless of students' economic circumstances.

AWARD THE BULK OF INSTITUTIONAL FINANCIAL AID ON THE BASIS OF NEED. Institutional aid should go to academically qualified but financially needy students, not to those whose families already can afford to pay.

No Turning Back the Clock but a Return to First Principles

This chapter has argued for a restoration of need-based principles of financial aid, or at least for stemming their erosion in public policy and campus practice. This is not to say that our society can go back to some halcyon era of student aid. As McPherson and Schapiro bring out in their research, there has always been a complex interplay and tension between meeting need and rewarding talent in American higher education. Even with the resolve and widespread impact of the 1954 compact that created CSS, scholarships offered without regard to need never disappeared. Many colleges continued to offer various forms of merit aid (and juggled the award of need-based assistance) to compete for the kind of students they deemed desirable.

Moreover, the concept of financial need and its measurement have been subject to disagreement right along. Need analysis is not science. In fact, its practical application has become increasingly problematic with changes in family structure, shifting enrollment patterns, and the older age profile of postsecondary students. More students are stretching out their education, studying part time, balancing academics with work and family responsibilities, going to college intermittently, or attending more than one institution before graduating.

The heart of the need-based aid tradition has been the assumption that parents have the primary obligation, to the limit of their ability, to pay for their children's education. But for growing numbers of older, self-supporting students, looking at parental finances is inappropriate or impractical. What to consider—how to judge relative need—when it comes to adult students in wide-ranging life circumstances is a far more complicated task than it was when the majority of students were age eighteen to twenty-two, dependent, and going to school full time.

So it is a more complicated world today, but that does not alter our society's fundamental obligation and challenge: to direct scarce resources in the most efficient and fairest way possible to equalize the opportunities for a college education in America.

Finally, it is well worth reiterating that financial aid is a necessary but insufficient condition for achieving the goal of equal opportunity. Access alone is not enough, nor is financial aid. To lift aspirations and the readiness of students for postsecondary education, complementary approaches are required. In sum, this country needs a much wider and deeper societal commitment to reaching, motivating, and preparing low-income students for college, as well as ensuring that price is not a barrier.

APPENDIX A

DEFINING TERMS:

COSTS, PRICES, AND SUBSIDIES IN HIGHER EDUCATION

In its 1998 report, "Straight Talk about College Costs and Prices," the National Commission on the Cost of Higher Education did a good job of clarifying terminology. It made a point of clearly distinguishing between expenditures that institutions make in order to provide education (which represent costs) and expenses that students and families face (prices). It also noted that what students pay is not the total cost of education. Indirect or general subsidies make it possible for institutions to charge less than the actual costs of instruction. State, federal, and local appropriations, as well as private philanthropy, reduce the prices faced by all students—whether or not they receive financial aid.

In this chapter, as in the commission's report, the terms "cost," "price," and "subsidy" are used as consistently as possible according to the following definitions:

* *COSTS:* What institutions spend to provide instruction and related educational services to students.

* *COST PER STUDENT:* The average amount spent annually to provide education and related services to each full-time-equivalent student.

* *PRICE:* What students and their families are charged, and what they pay.

* *STICKER OR PUBLISHED PRICE:* The tuition and fees that institutions charge.

* *TOTAL PRICE OF ATTENDANCE:* The tuition and fees that institutions charge students as well as related expenses. These expenses may include housing (room and board if the student lives on campus, or rent or related housing costs if the student does not live on campus), books, transportation, and incidentals. ("Price of attendance" is often referred to as the "cost of attendance.")

* *NET PRICE:* What students pay after financial aid—grants, loans, and work-study assistance—is subtracted from the total price of attendance.

* *INDIRECT OR GENERAL SUBSIDY:* The difference between the cost to the institution of providing educational services ("cost per student") and the tuition and fees charged to students ("sticker price"). Students who attend public or private, nonprofit higher education institutions typically receive a general subsidy. This indirect subsidy does not include support students receive from scholarships and other types of financial aid.

APPENDIX B
AN OVERVIEW OF PUBLISHED PRICES AND SUBSIDIES

PRICES

According to the College Board, average undergraduate tuition and fees in 2001–2002 were as follows:

Two-Year Public	$1,738
Two-Year Private	7,953
Four-Year Public	3,754
Four-Year Private	17,123

Posted tuition usually does not include room and board, transportation, books, supplies, and other education-related expenses such as laboratory fees. Estimated total expenses averaged as follows in 2001–2002:

Two-Year Public (commuter student)	$10,367
Two-Year Private (resident student)	15,755
Four-Year Public (resident student)	11,976
Four-Year Public (out-of-state student)	17,740
Four-Year Private (resident student)	26,070

INDIRECT SUBSIDIES

In 1995–96, according to the U.S. Department of Education, student tuition and fees paid for 19 percent of current fund revenues of public degree-granting institutions and 42 percent in the case of private, nonprofit degree-granting institutions. Other sources of revenue make it possible for institutions to charge less than the actual costs of instruction. Thus, virtually every student enrolled in these institutions receives a sizable indirect subsidy. State governments provide upward of $50 billion annually, or 37 percent, of revenues for public institutions. Private gifts and endowments account for 15 percent of revenues of private, nonprofit institutions.

DIRECT SUBSIDIES: STUDENT AID

According to the College Board, federal, state, institutional, and private sources provided more than $74 billion in student financial aid in 2000–2001. (See Figure 1.10; please note that these figures represent the amount of aid available to help students and families pay tuition, books and supplies, living and other expenses of attending higher education, not the revenues of institutions.) The federal government generated 68 percent of this aid, or $51 billion, $39–42 billion of which was in the form of borrowing. The states contributed 6 percent of direct student aid, mostly in the form of grants and scholarships. One-quarter of the state grants are awarded at least in part on academic merit, and this percentage is steadily increasing each year. Institutions contributed 20 percent of available aid. Another 6 percent came in the form of nonfederally sponsored student loans.

TUITION TAX RELIEF AND SAVINGS INCENTIVES

The Taxpayer Relief Act of 1997 included the Hope Scholarship and Lifetime Learning Tax Credit. The Hope Scholarship, in reality a tax credit rather than a scholarship, allows taxpayers to reduce their liability by up to $1,500 a year for tuition and fees paid during the first two years of postsecondary education. The Lifetime Learning Tax Credit provides an offset to tax liability of up to $2,000 for tuition and fees paid during any year of postsecondary education, undergraduate or graduate. The federal budget projects that the Hope Scholarship credit will cost the government $4.5 billion in lost revenue in 2003, while the Lifetime Learning Tax Credit will cost $3.0 billion.

The Economic Growth and Tax Relief Reconciliation Act of 2001 authorized a new above-the-line deduction for qualified higher education expenses. The maximum annual deduction starts at $3,000 and will rise to $4,000 in 2004. Tax expenditures for this provision are projected at $2.9 billion in 2003, rising to $4.8 billion in 2005.

Recent tax legislation also has created incentives for families to put money aside for their children's college expenses, with the earnings largely tax free. Section 529 savings plans, along with Education IRAs, are expected to cost more than $500 million in lost revenue in 2003 and well in excess of $1 billion in 2007.

Another tuition-related tax benefit is the deductibility of student loan interest, which had been abolished by the Tax Reform Act of 1986. It has now been restored and is projected to cost $760 million in revenue forgone in 2003.

For the above tuition tax benefits, it is projected that tax expenditures will total $11 billion in 2003 and a cumulative $60 billion for the five-year period 2003–2007.

Source: *Analytical Perspectives, Budget of the United States Government, Fiscal Year 2003*, Table 6-5: Outlay Equivalent Estimates for Tax Expenditures in the Income Tax, pp. 109–12, available online at http://w3.access.gpo.gov/usbudget/fy2003/pdf/spec.pdf.

2

IMPROVING THE ACADEMIC PREPARATION AND PERFORMANCE OF LOW-INCOME STUDENTS IN AMERICAN HIGHER EDUCATION

P. Michael Timpane and Arthur M. Hauptman

INTRODUCTION AND SUMMARY

TRENDS

For the past half century, American higher education has witnessed a remarkable expansion. The number of students in degree-granting programs has swelled tenfold, and the proportion of the population enrolled in any one year has grown fivefold since the end of the Second World War. While most of this increase had occurred by the mid-1970s, the number of students has risen by one-third since 1975—from 11 million to nearly 15 million—and the rate of participation has continued to go up as well, although not nearly as fast as in the period 1950–75.

Given these substantial overall increases in enrollments and participation rates, much of the concern about higher education in this country over the past several decades has focused on access: the fact that low-income and minority students have not shared equally in these gains. Low-income students are now roughly 50 percent more likely to enroll in college than they were three decades ago. But the growth in the proportion and number of students enrolling from the highest-income groups has been nearly as great. So the gap in terms of access between rich and poor has not materially narrowed since the federal role in education began in earnest in 1965 with the enactment of the two major pieces of federal education legislation: the Elementary and Secondary Education Act (ESEA) and the Higher Education Act (HEA).

The fulcrum of conversations on higher education in recent decades has been the issue of accessibility versus affordability. The accessibility discussion has explored how to assist low-income and minority students who lack the financial means to pay for the rapidly escalating costs of college, while affordability has become a code word for addressing middle-class concerns about such costs.

This chapter examines less well chronicled but equally important, complementary trends and developments for low-income students[1]—namely, how well they are prepared to do college-level work, how smooth or rough for them is the transition from high school to college, and how well they perform once they enroll in college, at least as measured by whether they attain degrees.

The available statistics indicate that improvements in the preparation and performance of American college students have not kept pace with whatever progress has been achieved in increasing their participation. The evidence also suggests that low-income students lag substantially behind students from families with greater means. Some of the most troubling statistics are enumerated here:

- The much-discussed achievement gap—the difference in test scores between low-income and minority students on the one hand and white and wealthier students on the other—persists and underscores the poor preparation of underprivileged students. Moreover, progress in closing the racial achievement gap made during the 1970s and 1980s has stalled in the past decade. A related concern is the growing number of students, particularly from low-income families, who require remedial work in order to perform satisfactorily at the college level.

- Degree completion rates in the United States appear to be average to below average among industrialized countries based on periodic longitudinal surveys. Less than half of the students who enroll in a higher education institution in the United States ever receive a degree.

◆   While the rate of degree completion is modest relative to other countries, educational attainment rates—the frequency with which Americans receive a degree—are among the highest in the world.[2] But the proportion of blacks and Hispanics twenty-five years of age or older who have earned a baccalaureate degree has consistently been about half that of whites for the past thirty years.

◆   Although there are no systematic data on trends in the proportion of students from low-income families who receive degrees, periodic surveys suggest this is a problem. For example, a survey of 1980 high school sophomores indicated that, twelve years later, those from poor families were three times less likely to attain a bachelor's degree than middle-class students and six times less likely than students from wealthy families.[3]

These concerns about the levels of preparation and performance of low-income students tie in directly to the principal points of contention in education policy over the past several decades. In K–12 education, school reform and the development and implementation of higher standards for students have been prime issues. A distinctive and controversial feature of this debate has been the insistence that all students—especially those from backgrounds of poverty and other sources of deprivation—must be held to high standards and expectations. Many fear that these quality and equity concerns have not been well matched and that low-income and minority students will find it even harder than other students to meet rising standards.

Higher education policy needs a much greater balance between the goals of improving preparation, participation, and performance of low-income students. Increasing participation, the dominant goal of federal higher education policy as it concerns low-income students for the past three decades, is an absolutely necessary but ultimately insufficient condition of their success. Increasing participation must be part of a coordinated set of higher education policies that pay much greater attention to issues of readiness for college and achievement as well.

PROBLEMS

The imbalance between preparation, participation, and performance is attributable to a traditional lack of governmental focus on how students actually fare in college, poor targeting of benefits on low-income students, ineffective system design, and lopsided funding priorities. Each of these policy failings is considered in turn.

LACK OF POLICY FOCUS ON PREPARATION AND PERFORMANCE. It should not be surprising that the most progress in tackling the higher education needs of low-income students over the past half century has come in the area of participation because that is where most of the policy attention and the funding historically have been focused. Much less energy at both the federal and state level has been devoted to ensuring that students are ready to deal with the academic challenges of college and can complete their program of study once enrolled.

Major policies and programs encourage participation without regard for, and sometimes at the expense of, performance. Most states through their funding formula reward institutions on the basis of the number of students who enroll in the fall, not the number who complete the year in the spring or who graduate. Federal student aid policies are notoriously lax in enforcing any legislative or regulatory requirement that student beneficiaries achieve satisfactorily to continue receiving aid.

LACK OF TARGETING. Even when their stated intent is to serve the needs of the poor, most public policies and programs in higher education principally benefit the middle class or do not have a particularly effective focus on the poor. Low tuition at public institutions has been the principal access-oriented policy of states, but this is a very ineffective way of targeting the neediest students because the subsidy keeps tuition charges low for all enrolled students. This is a particular problem at public flagship universities, where most students are from high- rather than low-income families. Student aid has been the primary federal policy to broaden access, but it, too, is not very well honed as political pressures have caused Washington to provide an increasing share of benefits to financially independent students or those from middle-income families.

Similarly, higher education programs and policies that focus on precollegiate education such as teacher preparation typically are designed to improve the skills of all students and do not concentrate on helping teachers meet the special learning needs of low-income students. This is the case even though students from poorer backgrounds historically are more likely to go into teaching than students from wealthier families.

INEFFECTIVE SYSTEM DESIGN. Public policies and programs at both the federal and state levels are neither well designed nor coordinated effectively to encourage better preparation or performance of low-income students. For example, the admission guidelines that most higher education institutions use are not tied or related to the standards used to determine high school graduation or the tests used to measure progress in K–12 education.

Similarly, the federal student aid programs for a quarter century have been available to students who have not received a high school degree or its equivalent. While this enhances access, it also increases the number of students who require remediation and who often must borrow to pay for the remedial courses they need. The expansion of open admission universities and community colleges, so instrumental in providing greater access to American higher education, has not been as conducive to stimulating or reinforcing the preparedness of students entering higher education. In short, the programs are designed to enhance access rather than to be concerned with questions of access to what, or to what avail.

LOPSIDED FUNDING PRIORITIES. Funding levels are another way in which priorities are expressed. In the case of higher education, student aid has taken the lion's share of federal spending. A very small proportion of federal and state funding is directed at support services or early intervention efforts such as the new federal Gaining Early Awareness and Readiness for Undergraduate Programs (GEAR-UP). Similarly, at the state level, direct support for public institutions, the predominant form of higher education assistance in the United States, favors participation since it is based on the number of students enrolled. There are few sizable state programs for either institutions or students that focus on low-income populations or on performance.

THE NEED FOR AN INTEGRATIVE APPROACH

Public policies and institutional practices at all points along the educational pipeline must be reformed and better aligned if higher levels of preparation and performance by low-income students in higher education are to be achieved. This chapter focuses on what changes in higher education policies and practices can be made to achieve these purposes at three stages in the educational process: K–12 education; the transition from high school to college; and student progress once they enroll in college.

K–12 EDUCATION FOR LOW-INCOME STUDENTS MAY BE IMPROVED BY:

◆   Encouraging the creation and expansion of academic partner-
    ships between schools and universities;

◆   Strengthening the focus of teacher preparation and professional
    development programs on serving low-income populations.

*THE HIGH SCHOOL TO COLLEGE TRANSITION FOR THOSE FROM POORER
BACKGROUNDS CAN BE STRENGTHENED BY:*

◆   Expanding funding of precollegiate support services and early
    intervention programs;

◆   Encouraging greater alignment between high school graduation
    requirements and college admissions standards;

•   Redesigning the delivery and financing of remedial coursework.

*THE PERFORMANCE OF STUDENTS OF CONCERN ENROLLED IN COLLEGE
SHOULD RESPOND FAVORABLY TO:*

◆   Provision of sustained mentoring and support services once stu-
    dents enroll;

◆   Redesign of student aid programs to target assistance more accu-
    rately on low-income students and to encourage greater persis-
    tence and performance;

◆   Modification of state funding formulas to reward institutions
    for enrolling and graduating low-income students.

    While this list presents an ambitious agenda for reform, it is not
necessarily an expensive one. Most of these reforms build upon existing programs and can be achieved either through reallocation of
resources or relatively small incremental additions because the activities proposed for expansion do not currently command a sizable
share of funding for higher education. Spending on early intervention is a small fraction of what the government spends on students.
For example, GEAR-UP costs less than 5 percent of federal spending

on Pell Grants.[4] Similarly, designating more student aid funds for low-income students need not depend on greater expenditures on financial assistance overall but could entail a reallocation of funds or subsidies now flowing to many affluent students.

One exception to this rule of no or little cost increase would be a proposed change in the way remediation is funded: not charging tuition and not allowing students to borrow for these courses. This proposal would save money in student loan interest subsidies and reduced defaults but could cost considerably more in the process of underwriting the operating expenses for these courses. The societal investment would be well worth the additional cost if it were to break the cycle of growing debt burdens and defaults being incurred by poorly prepared students who come from low-income families. Moreover, by way of compensation it would remove the costs of failing to educate these students in the first place, especially students who have received high school diplomas but still lack critical basic skills.

TRENDS IN PREPARATION, PARTICIPATION, PERFORMANCE, AND OUTCOMES

This section reviews historical trends in a series of indicators relating to the academic preparation, participation, and performance of students in American higher education, particularly for students from low-income families to the extent data are available. Indicators reviewed include:

+ High school dropout and graduation rates;

+ College preparation levels;

+ Higher education participation rates;

+ Academic performance while in college;

+ Degree completion and attainment rates.

HIGH SCHOOL DROPOUT AND GRADUATION RATES. Table 2.1 (page 67) indicates that the rate at which low-income students drop out from high school has declined modestly in the past thirty years (from 28 to 21 percent). Dropout rates have narrowed considerably between blacks and whites, from fifteen to five percentage points in thirty years, but Hispanic dropout rates remain twenty percentage points higher than for whites. The high school dropout rate for low-income students remains five to six times as great as for the highest-income group, the same as thirty years ago.

As Table 2.1 also indicates, the proportional difference in high school graduation rates between white and black students has narrowed dramatically (from 23 to 7 percentage points) over the past three decades, but the difference between whites and Hispanics has remained in excess of 25 percentage points. In one recent year, the high school graduation rate for the highest-income group was roughly 50 percent larger than that of the lowest income group (90 percent versus 60 percent).[5]

COLLEGE PREPARATION LEVELS. There are, as far as can be discerned, no measures of the achievement levels over time of high school graduates by family income. The closest available measure is SAT scores— a nonrepresentative sample—for which, for more than thirty years, the combined verbal and math scores of students with family incomes in the lowest 10–15 percent of test takers have lagged approximately two hundred points behind the scores of students from the top 10–15 percent in family income.[6]

Recently, in 1998 and again in 2002, the National Assessment of Educational Programs (NAEP) has reported reading scores broken out by eligibility for free/reduced-price lunch, with similar patterns of disparity for twelfth graders in both of those years—the average reading achievement scores of eligible twelfth-grade students are almost identical to the scores of eighth graders who do not qualify for free or reduced-price lunch.[7]

There are numerous studies that demonstrate a chronic achievement gap by race and ethnicity. After narrowing from 1970 to 1988, the gap has stabilized since, such that the reading proficiency scores of black and Hispanic seventeen-year-olds in the NAEP as reported in Table 2.1 are approximately equal to those of white and Asian thirteen-year-olds.[8] There is a strong but complex relationship among racial/ethnic characteristics, family income, and educational achievement. The majority of low-income students are, after all, not minorities. And yet, minority status, not just family income, accounts for some part of the disparity in student performance.[9]

TABLE 2.1 SELECTED PREPARATION, PARTICIPATION, AND EDUCATIONAL ATTAINMENT TRENDS

	2000 (est.)	1995	1990	1985	1980	1975	1970	1965	1960	1950	1940
POPULATION (in millions)											
Total Population	273	263	250	238	228	216	205	194	181	152	132
Ages 16–24 years	34.1	32.5	33.8	36.5	38.8	36.5	32.5	27.2	21.8	20.2	21.5

PRE-COLLEGIATE TRENDS

HIGH SCHOOL DROPOUT RATES (as a percentage of 16–24 year olds) *

	1999	1995	1990	1985	1980	1975	1970
All	11.2	12.0	12.1	12.6	14.1	13.9	15.0
BY FAMILY INCOME QUARTILE *							
Lowest	21.0	23.2	24.3	27.1	27.0	28.8	28.0
Middle-low	14.3	13.8	15.1	14.7	18.1	18.0	21.2
Middle-high	7.4	8.3	8.7	8.3	10.7	10.2	11.7
Highest	3.9	3.6	2.9	4.0	5.7	5.0	5.2
BY RACE/ETHNICITY *							
White	7.3	8.6	9.0	10.4	11.4	11.4	13.2
Black	12.6	12.1	13.2	15.2	19.1	22.9	27.9
Hispanic	28.6	30.0	32.4	27.6	35.2	29.2	na

Continued

TABLE 2.1   SELECTED PREPARATION,
PARTICIPATION, AND EDUCATIONAL ATTAINMENT TRENDS (CONTINUED)

High School Graduation Rates (as percentage of 25–29 year olds who have completed high school)**

	2000	1995	1990	1985	1980	1975	1970
All	88	87	86	86	85	83	78
White	94	93	90	90	89	87	82
Black	87	87	82	81	77	71	59
Hispanic	63	57	58	61	58	53	48

Reading Proficiency (as percentage of 17 year olds above level 250)**

	1999	1995	1990	1985	1980	1975	1971
All	82	80	84	83	81	80	79
White	87	86	88	88	87	86	84
Black	66	66	69	66	44	43	40
Hispanic	68	64	75	68	62	53	na

HIGHER EDUCATION TRENDS

Higher Education Enrollments +

	2000	1995	1990	1985	1980	1975	1970	1965	1960	1950	1940
All higher ed (in millions)	15.0	14.3	13.8	12.2	12.1	11.1	8.6	5.9	4.0	2.3	1.5
as % of total population	5.5	5.4	5.5	5.1	5.3	5.1	4.2	3.0	2.2	1.5	1.1
as % of 16–24 population	44.0	44.0	41.0	33.0	31.0	30.0	26.0	22.0	18.0	11.0	7.0
Community Colleges (in millions)	5.5	5.3	5	4.3	4.3	3.8	2.2	1.0	0.4	0.1	na
as % of all higher education	37.0	37.0	36.0	35.0	36.0	34.0	26.0	17.0	10.0	4.0	na

TABLE 2.1 SELECTED PREPARATION,
PARTICIPATION, AND EDUCATIONAL ATTAINMENT TRENDS (CONTINUED)

ENROLLMENT RATES OF RECENT HIGH SCHOOL GRADUATES ++

	2000	1995	1990	1985	1980	1975	1972
All	63	62	60	58	49	51	49
By income							
High income	77	77	77	75	65	65	64
Middle income	59	56	54	51	43	46	45
Low income	50	42	45	36	32	31	26
By ethnic/racial status							
White	66	63	62	59	50	51	52
Black	55	51	46	42	42	42	45
Hispanic	49	51	53	47	50	48	45

ATTAINMENT: (percentage of 25–29-year olds who have completed 4 or more years of college) ^

	2000	1995	1990	1985	1980	1975	1970
Total	33	28	27	26	27	26	22
White	36	31	30	27	29	28	23
Black	21	18	14	14	17	15	12
Hispanic	15	16	16	18	13	17	11

Continued

TABLE 2.1 SELECTED PREPARATION,
PARTICIPATION, AND EDUCATIONAL ATTAINMENT TRENDS (CONTINUED)

* *Source:* National Center for Education Statistics, *Digest of Education Statistics, 2000* (Washington, D.C.: U.S. Department of Education, 2001), Table 107.

** *Source:* National Center for Education Statistics, *The Condition of Education, 2000* (Washington, D.C.: U.S. Department of Education, June 2000), Table 113.

+ *Source:* National Center for Education Statistics, *Digest of Education Statistics, 1998* (Washington, D.C.: U.S. Department of Education, 1999), Table 172.

++ *Source:* National Center for Education Statistics, *The Condition of Education, 2003* (Washington, D.C.: U.S. Department of Education, June 2003), Table 18-1.

^ *Source:* National Center for Education Statistics, *The Condition of Education, 2000* (Washington, D.C.: U.S. Department of Education, June 2000), Table 113.

Another way to view the readiness issue is to examine the proportion of college entrants who are prepared to do the work. Although there are no systematic data, institution-based reports suggest that low-income students are much more likely to require remediation than students from higher-income families. In one longitudinal survey, only half of 1992 low-income high school graduates who qualified for admission at a four-year institution were minimally qualified to enroll, compared to more than four-fifths of higher-income ($75,000 or more) students. Of perhaps greater concern, only one-fifth of the low-income high school graduates were highly qualified, compared to nearly three-fifths of the high-income students.[10]

HIGHER EDUCATION PARTICIPATION RATES. To get a fuller perspective on progress in improving higher education participation rates, it is worthwhile to examine trends stretching back to the end of the Second World War. The reason for this longer time frame lies in the tremendous changes in American higher education that have occurred over the past half century. As Table 2.1 indicates, enrollments in American higher education increased fourfold from 1940 to 1965, when the major pieces of federal legislation were enacted. Enrollments doubled again between 1965 and 1980 and have increased by a more modest but still substantial 25 percent since 1980.

The higher education participation rate in the United States, measured by the number of college students as a proportion of the total population, shows similar growth, increasing fivefold from 1940 to 1975, with only modest increases since. For the traditional college-age population, participation rates have steadily grown throughout and now are at all-time highs, with more than two-thirds of high school graduates continuing schooling in the following year.

With regard to differences among income groups, the higher education participation rates of low-income students doubled from one-quarter to one-half between 1970 and the mid-1990s. During the same time, participation rates for high-income students increased from two-thirds to four-fifths. Thus, the gap in participation rates between rich and poor has narrowed some but remains substantial.

ACADEMIC PERFORMANCE IN COLLEGE. Unfortunately, there are neither accepted measures nor comprehensive assessments of academic performance in higher education, let alone comparisons by income status. Given the conceptual, methodological, and political hurdles involved, this situation is unlikely to change anytime soon.[11]

DEGREE COMPLETION AND EDUCATIONAL ATTAINMENT. Degree completion rates (graduates as a proportion of initial entrants) in the United States appear to be average to below average among industrialized countries. There are no systematic trend data to confirm this; thus, any assessment must be based on periodic surveys. For example, based on a longitudinal survey of 1980 high school sophomores, more than 90 percent graduated from high school, but only one-fifth received a baccalaureate by 1992.[12] Based on the same survey, students from the lowest quartile of socioeconomic status were three times less likely to attain a bachelor's degree than middle-income students and six times less likely than high-income students.[13]

Educational attainment in the United States, by contrast, remains among the highest in the world, with more than one-quarter of twenty-five- to twenty-nine-year-olds in the population completing four or more years of college (see Table 2.1). But the proportion of blacks and Hispanics twenty-five years of age or older who receive a baccalaureate degree has consistently been a little more than half that of whites. There appear to be no trend data on educational attainment by student family income, in large part because family income is not viewed as being relevant when looking at individuals who are twenty-five years old or older.

POSSIBLE CONTRIBUTORS TO PREPARATION AND PERFORMANCE TRENDS

To investigate the possible linkage among policies and trends in preparation and performance, this section examines higher education policies and programs that affect low-income students at three points in the educational pipeline: the precollegiate level, the transition from high school to college, and the period when students are actually enrolled in college.

- In terms of students at the precollegiate level, this section reflects on higher education's efforts (or lack thereof) in the school reform movement of the past twenty years, the impact of its teacher preparation efforts, and the wide range of partnership arrangements established between K–12 systems and postsecondary institutions.

◆ In terms of policies and programs that affect students during the transition from high school to college, the tenuous connection between new high school graduation requirements arising out of the school reform movement and college admissions standards are considered here as well as the role of early intervention and mentoring programs and policies for financing remediation.

◆ With regard to students' achievement once they reach higher education, the policies examined include state support of public institutions, creation and expansion of access-oriented institutions such as community colleges, government-funded student aid programs, and tax incentives for students and their families.

HIGHER EDUCATION'S ROLE IN IMPROVING K–12 EDUCATION

For the past two decades, the national debate over improving K–12 education has been dominated by issues of school reform and the development and implementation of high-standards programs for students, accompanied by new assessments and accountability provisions. A distinctive and controversial feature of this reform has been its insistence that *all* students—especially those from backgrounds of poverty or other sorts of deprivation—must be held to these high standards and expectations.

Clearly, this reform agenda has immense implications for higher education and for the postsecondary prospects of low-income students. Nevertheless, higher education's participation in K–12 reforms has been episodic and mostly reactive—far more limited than, for example, the interest and involvement of the corporate sector or state governors. Very little attention has been given to any direct implications of the school reforms for higher education's own policies and practices.

For generations, higher education's policies and practices have profoundly influenced K–12 education, especially the high school. A group dominated by college presidents (the Committee of 12) set the basic high school curriculum more than a century ago, by converting classical academies into institutions that taught math, science, history, and English.

Not long after, early in the twentieth century, the Carnegie Foundation for the Advancement of Teaching invented the Carnegie unit as the basic descriptor of the academic courses in high school curricula. Subsequently, its parent, the Carnegie Corporation, helped establish the College Entrance Examination Board, the Education Testing Service (ETS), and the Scholastic Aptitude Test (SAT). These instruments—the Carnegie unit and the SAT—both developed at the behest of higher education, dominated college admissions decisions in most institutions for most of the century that followed. Few high schools dared stray from the academic program they implied.

After the Second World War, President James B. Conant of Harvard extended the influence of higher education again, lauding the then-emerging comprehensive high school model, placing the college prep curriculum alongside vocational and other programs in the same large institution. Conant noted, even then, that developments (poverty and race) in the nation's cities were likely to frustrate his larger objectives.

Finally, in the wake of Sputnik, higher education weighed in yet again, stressing the need for stronger math and science curricula, aimed mostly at the then relatively small proportion of students who were college-bound, and developed mostly by university professors.

Ironically, even while this curricular hegemony grew, higher education and K–12 systems drew steadily apart. Many of the growing mass education and social development responsibilities of the schools were of little or no interest to those in higher education, whose move to a research orientation widened the intellectual gap even further. Many professors in the university disdained their colleagues in the colleges of education and in the schools. Many professors in the colleges of education themselves declined to have much contact with the schools. And many teachers in the schools derided their own preparation as well as those who inflicted it upon them. Moreover, as public higher education institutions and systems expanded, their governance at the state level was organized and carried on with little or no connection to the K–12 systems.

Thus, higher education, notwithstanding its dominant historical influence, was and is ill equipped by experience or inclination to be a major participant in the contemporary reform of K–12 education that would surely influence deeply its own future. Major new issues, though, compel its expanded attention and participation in efforts to improve the situation of low-income students in the K–12 system, including:

1. The new K–12 academic standards—which face their greatest challenge and opportunity in their application to youngsters from low-income and minority backgrounds—must be articulated with higher education admissions standards. In the estimation of parents and students, postsecondary education has become, for good or ill, the universal passport to the good life. If higher education does not reinforce primary and secondary school standards in its admissions and academic programs, the K–12 reform is unlikely to succeed, and poor youth are likely to be left even further behind.

2. Advanced Placement (AP) and International Baccalaureate (IB) programs are proliferating. These AP and IB courses may help or hurt low-income students, depending upon the nature and extent of their participation. If, as seems likely, participation and performance patterns correlate with other measures of curricular rigor and achievement, these courses could lead to a new kind of academic tracking and relative disadvantage for low-income students seeking to enter higher education.

3. Similarly, the high-stakes graduation tests now in place in a growing number of states (twenty-two at last count) will, initially at least, have a disproportionately adverse impact on low-income students.

4. With the expanded numbers of higher education entrants requiring remedial help, higher education and the K–12 system must develop shared objectives and collaborative programs rather than squabble over blame and responsibilities.

As suggested, higher education has not often taken the initiative in supporting K–12 improvement efforts, which were mostly on behalf of low-income students. Few college presidents were in the vanguard of recent policy reforms (in contrast to earlier days), and university officials were often fearful that the expansion of K–12 programs would come at higher education's expense. Higher education faculty did little in their academic norms and attitudes to encourage or reward colleagues who did their research and service in or for schools.

As the school reform movement has proceeded and has gradually come to dominate K–12 education policy development, several aspects of higher education policy and practices have come into focus, including but not limited to the strengthening of teacher preparation programs and the expansion of a wide-ranging set of activities to strengthen local K–12 programs (often termed "K–16 partnerships").

TEACHER PREPARATION. Clearly, one of higher education's most obvious opportunities to strengthen its sustained contribution to the education of low-income students at every level of education lies in its preparation of almost all of the 300,000 teachers who enter our K–12 schools each year.[14] The large majority of these new teachers receive their professional degrees (bachelor's or master's) in schools or colleges of education; most of these, in turn, take much of their coursework, and often their bachelor's degree, in liberal arts programs.

These teachers-in-preparation undoubtedly include sizable proportions of low-income students; public school teachers have long been drawn from working-class or lower-middle-class families and have often been among the first in their families to attend college. For most of the twentieth century, moreover, women and minorities had few other professions open to them and thus contributed hugely and disproportionately to the nation's stock of talented teachers.

With expansion of college enrollments and professional opportunity in other fields, K–12 education is no longer the principal opportunity for low-income, minority, and female students to make professional progress, but it is still the largest single source of jobs for college graduates, if only at modest salaries. This group of college graduates is surely the most likely to provide sustained, direct service to the next generation of poor and minority students. If tomorrow's teachers—from modest means themselves—are to be more well prepared to succeed with low-income students, it will be because higher education's teacher preparation programs have taught them how to do so. Unfortunately, higher education may not be suitably equipped to step up to this challenge.

◆   Education schools and programs are not high priority or high in prestige on most campuses. Specific presidents and deans have taken on the task of strengthening these schools, but most have not. There has been little pressure from within or without for most leaders to do so. More prestigious fields (medicine, law, business) or more highly valued activity (like research and consulting) vie successfully for resources, fame, and institutional attention and support. Education programs have been, in too many cases, simply convenient repositories for large numbers of students who make few academic demands and contribute steady income.

♦   Measuring the quality of specific teacher education programs has been difficult and highly controversial. Various review, award, and recognition programs (for example, the new standards of the National Commission on Accreditation of Teacher Education [NCATE] and Congress's recent requirement that education programs receiving federal support demonstrate that high proportions [70 percent] of their graduates pass state certification exams) have attempted to do so with mixed and limited success. Many researchers studying teacher preparation programs have discerned modest positive effects on learning and a clear set of attributes for strong programs, but even these findings are hotly debated by skeptics.[15] And little attention is given in any of these analyses to effectiveness in educating low-income students.

♦   Within most teacher preparation programs, little emphasis has been given to preparing new teachers to succeed with the special needs and challenges posed by low-income children—except where geography and mission make such emphasis inevitable, as at many urban public institutions and historically black colleges and universities.[16]

Along each of these dimensions there are promising developments upon which more can be built. The nation's teacher educators have been struggling for almost two decades to redesign and strengthen their programs—adding requirements for disciplinary knowledge, clinical experience, and professional subjects. In the creation of the National Board for Professional Teaching Standards they have worked toward defining and rewarding true excellence among teachers. Through NCATE they have set up new national standards for professional accreditation containing, for first time, provisions for focus on teaching poor and minority students. In the invention of professional development schools and of organized programs for teacher induction during their first years in the classroom, they have begun to revolutionize the nature and extent of clinical preparation. In these and in myriad new professional development partnerships, they have rebuilt relationships of mutual service with practitioners. They have begun to strengthen ties with disciplinary faculties, notably mathematics, in devising new programs of preparation and instruction. They need more support, though, from higher education leaders and more focus from policymakers on their vital role in closing the achievement gap in our schools, as well as careful evaluation of their effectiveness, particularly with regard to teaching low-income students.

K–16 PARTNERSHIPS. Over the past two decades colleges and universities have begun slowly to build new relationships with local school systems, emphasizing the ways they can strengthen programs and communities. These partnerships use university resources to help improve instruction and other activities, usually in local schools; sometimes they promote more general policies and practices beneficial to K–12 education. Taken together, these initiatives have focused on the problems or prospects of low-income students and represent a gradual but hardly revolutionary increase in the relative priority of K–12 (or K–16) issues on college and university campuses.

Such partnership programs by now are present on almost every college campus, often with the encouragement of presidents who are giving them greater priority and resources. Typically, they involve some limited number of faculty, staff or students in a specific activity, such as mentoring, course development, or community-based activity. These programs are prominent and numerous on many campuses but are rarely of a scale to improve whole systems or even entire schools.[17] The past few years have seen the first attempts to systematize such partnerships at the state level, providing policy mandates and incentives for state-sponsored joint activities to foster ongoing collaborations between localities and institutions.[18]

STRENGTHENING THE TRANSITION FROM HIGH SCHOOL TO COLLEGE

Education policy debates in this country have tended to move on two separate tracks. The issues debated with regard to K–12 education are remarkably disjoined from the issues of concern in higher education circles. This difference is reflected at the federal level by the existence of two entirely distinct bodies of legislation for elementary and secondary education on the one hand and higher education on the other, enacted in the same year, 1965, as integral parts of President Johnson's War on Poverty but embodying disparate policies, strategies, and programs. State education policies also typically move on separate tracks. Similarly, very few educational policymakers or analysts play significant roles in the debates over both K–12 and higher education.

One unfortunate manifestation of the separation between K–12 and higher education policies is that the critical transition period between these educational levels has suffered neglect. Over time far too little attention has been paid in public policy debates at federal and state levels to the problems entailed in moving from high school to college. This lack of focus on the transition period is particularly of concern for low-income students, who typically face substantially more difficult obstacles in making the jump. Some of these problems are: the lack of alignment between high school graduation requirements and college admissions standards; the need to raise aspirations of low-income students; and the development and financing of remedial courses for students admitted to higher education ill prepared to progress academically.

HIGH SCHOOL GRADUATION REQUIREMENTS AND COLLEGE ADMISSIONS STANDARDS. The record of colleges and universities in admitting low-income students is one of considerable accomplishment; these students attend in significantly greater numbers than their tested levels of academic preparation would suggest. Nevertheless, higher education has two admissions problems that limit the retention and academic progress of low-income students:

◆   for many institutions, admission standards are too low, allowing many ill-prepared students (disproportionately underprivileged) to enroll, leading to a burgeoning need for remediation, high dropout rates, and, not incidentally, substantial levels of debt for students who are still poorly educated and still poor. Such low standards in higher education also undercut K–12 efforts to hold all students to high levels of performance;

◆   for all types of institutions, admissions criteria, where they have real substance, are not often aligned to the standards being set in place in most states' K–12 systems. SAT and ACT tests, for example, are not so aligned, nor is class rank in high school, another commonly used criterion.

An obvious step but one rarely taken is for higher education admissions and K–12 standards to be developed and implemented in tandem, to the benefit of both. There are important precedents in the K–16 initiatives of a few states, notably, Oregon, Maryland, and Georgia.[19] These initiatives, building on the standards-based K–12 reforms emerging in these (and most other) states, seek to change secondary school programs in directions that are consistent with reforms in college admissions standards and processes, in some cases with a particular focus on the preparation and progress of low-income students. They are, by all accounts, incredibly difficult to sustain without ample resources and strong political support. Nothing in the history or governance of either higher or primary and secondary education promotes such intensive collaboration; the contemporary politics of education seldom requires it, and college presidents and school superintendents have rarely been rewarded or punished for what they did or did not do in cooperating with each other.

Some promising new initiatives are grappling with this problem directly, with a focus on the underlying issues of academic readiness:

◆   The American Diploma Project—sponsored by Achieve, the Fordham Foundation, the National Alliance of Business, and the Education Trust—is supporting five states (Nevada, Texas, Indiana, Massachusetts, and Kentucky) in the creation of explicit, comprehensive, statewide correspondence of standards for high school graduation and college admissions;

◆   The Bill and Melinda Gates Foundation has launched an initiative creating fifty or more "early colleges" aimed at accelerating student achievement through high school and the first two years of college, especially for poor and minority students;

◆   More than thirty "middle colleges"—small high schools situated on community college campuses—also target low-income students.

Such pressures from above and below may begin to create a new consensus among schools and colleges about the form and substance of shared academic standards.

SUPPORT SERVICES AND EARLY INTERVENTION. Since 1965 the TRIO programs have represented the principal federal effort to provide a range of support services to low-income and at-risk students before they reach college and while they are enrolled. They do so largely through discretionary grants to colleges and universities and other nonprofit organizations that run one or several of the TRIO programs—Upward Bound, Talent Search, Special Services, and Educational Opportunity Centers.[20]

The TRIO programs are generally regarded as an example of a federal effort that works, although relatively few evaluations have been conducted of these programs since they were enacted.[21] The three hundred to four hundred institutions that annually receive TRIO funding usually get good grades for their programs. Educational Opportunity Centers have become a mainstay in many poor communities, providing a reliable clearinghouse on college and financial aid opportunities for groups of low-income students and their families, who typically are given far too little of this critical information.

But after more than three decades of operation, the TRIO programs still reach less than 10 percent of the eligible population of at-risk students, and there has been little push from the federal government or higher education officials to move them from demonstration programs to a full-scale, national effort at the high school and collegiate level. Moreover, TRIO does not as a rule make much of a connection with grade schools and middle schools, which is where the available research and common sense indicate that public and private efforts must penetrate if more adequate preparation of at-risk students is to be achieved.

There is a growing recognition among educators that a fuller range of such services—providing motivation, information, and support—is a necessary complement to well-funded student aid programs to ensure greater access and success in higher education for at-risk populations.[22] Similarly, in the past two decades the focus of this non-student aid component of federal higher education policy has shifted somewhat to trying to reach at-risk students in grade school and middle school rather than waiting until high school and college as in the TRIO programs. This shift was occasioned in part by the success of private ventures such as Eugene Lang's well-publicized "I Have a Dream" program, begun in the 1980s, in which philanthropists and corporations adopted grade school classes in poor neighborhoods and provided them with the assurance of financial aid if they were admitted to college and with a set of mentoring and support services to help ensure they were ready. Many of these private efforts have had remarkable results, with a large majority of the students involved graduating from high school and enrolling and completing college.[23]

In an effort to institutionalize these private successes as a matter of public policy, the 1992 reauthorization of the Higher Education Act contained a small matching program designed to encourage states to establish early intervention programs of their own. The 1998 reauthorization of the HEA took a much bigger step on the road toward recognizing the importance of early intervention with the passage of GEAR-UP. This is a much-expanded early intervention effort consisting of a series of incentives for colleges and universities to form partnerships with middle schools and school systems to provide counseling, mentoring, and increased financial aid opportunities for at-risk students, while at the same time it incorporates and expands the state-based incentive approach enacted in 1992.

By focusing on providing support services in high school and college and early intervention in grade school and middle school, GEAR-UP represents a broadened federal strategy aimed at improving preparation and performance of low-income students in higher education. But what is the evidence on how effective this new federal program is likely to be in improving the college preparation and performance of such students?

Private efforts such as "I Have a Dream" receive very good grades on their ability to reach students early and to improve the preparation and raise the aspirations of students who otherwise would have little real chance of going to college or handling the workload once there. This notion of raising the aspirations of high at-risk students builds on Senator Claiborne Pell's aspiration that economically disadvantaged grade school students would be assured of a substantial amount of college aid to motivate them to do well in school. But the initial promise of Pell Grants has never been realized because the program never become a fully funded entitlement program, and federal budget rules have been interpreted to preclude promising aid to individuals more than one year in advance.

The idea of adopting a whole class of grade school students, providing mentoring and counseling, and promising adequate financial aid really seems to have worked in the case of "I Have A Dream" and similar efforts, as evidenced by as many as 90 percent of the class going to college and an equally impressive percentage completing their degree. But such programs are no substitute for public policy, inasmuch as they bestow large benefits on small, selected groups of students.

The success thus far of government early intervention has been more limited than the private ventures. Only a handful of states picked up on the incentives contained in the 1992 program, and GEAR-UP is really too new to make much of a judgment. But if enthusiasm counts, then GEAR-UP is already a success, as many hundreds of institutions have applied for its grants in its first two years of operation.

Both TRIO and GEAR-UP seem to be reasonably well targeted on low-income students. An important problem for both programs seems to be inadequate funding and reach, which has prevented TRIO from becoming much more than a demonstration program and has hindered GEAR-UP's efforts to sponsor many worthy applicants in its early years. Thus, a good first step in the effort to improve preparation and raise aspirations would be the expansion of both TRIO and GEAR-UP to reach most if not all low-income students who seek a college education. Meeting full eligibility would cost several billion dollars, but doubling the funding of both TRIO and GEAR-UP (collectively they currently are allocated about $1 billion) would do a lot.

Another important step would be to examine the program design to determine what features may have contributed to the stunted growth of TRIO and what aspects of GEAR-UP require modification to allow for improved effectiveness. In the case of GEAR-UP, any reorganization would build on the commitment in the enabling legislation to evaluate the effects of the funded partnerships between higher education institutions and middle schools and school systems and to change their terms as needed.

REMEDIATION. One of the underpinnings of the initial HEA legislation was that eligibility for student financial aid was conditioned on the students graduating from high school, prepared to do college-level work. But since 1976 students without a high school diploma or equivalency degree have been able to receive all forms of federal student financial aid if they can demonstrate an "ability to benefit" from such assistance. While this legislative change has expanded educational opportunities for millions of students over the past quarter century, the tests used to demonstrate the required "ability to benefit" have been notoriously suspect, often developed and administered by the institutions themselves. There also can be little doubt that these provisions have added greatly to the need for remediation among a growing number of college-age students.

This seems to be particularly true of low-income students who qualify for the most aid as a result of these provisions. The most notorious examples are the many stories of fly-by-night institutions recruiting poor students off the streets to enroll in their programs, using federal student aid as their principal recruitment tool.

But concern about remediation is not limited to the apparent growth in the number of underprepared students entering college or to the sensationalized accounts of predatory recruitment practices by marginal schools. Through a range of policies and practices, from recruitment and admissions to support services and curricular adaptations, many individual colleges and universities make extensive and laudable efforts to help underprepared students successfully pursue higher education. But how successful are these remedial efforts in improving the degree completion rates of low-income students?

The intense debate over the role and results of remediation has been one generating more heat than light. There have been few if any rigorous evaluations of the effectiveness of different remedial approaches in raising preparation levels, particularly whether technology is meeting one of its main promises of improving learning outcomes for at-risk populations. The most contentious debate instead has focused on the level of remediation needed and whether institutions are being adequately compensated by states and localities for the costs of providing remedial courses.

This brings us to perhaps the most objectionable aspect of current student aid policy, one that best reflects the high degree of disconnect between higher education and K–12 systems: the extensive use of loans to finance remedial studies in courses that do not qualify as college level. Students taking remedial courses typically pay full tuition for them and are fully eligible for the range of federal aid programs. As a result, many of these students are paying tuition and borrowing substantially to finance the acquisition of skills that they should have received for free in K–12 education. To the extent that they are less likely to complete their studies and get a decent job, they disproportionately default on their student loans. While this unfortunate situation occurs with greatest frequency among low-income students enrolled in trade schools, many underprepared students matriculated in academic programs in a wide range of institutions are equally or more adversely affected.

This problem could be solved by taking two related steps: first, not charging tuition for remedial courses; second, not allowing students to borrow to pay for the remedial courses they take, although needy students would still be eligible for Pell Grants to help pay for their living expenses. Remediation is not really college-level work, and these two proposals recognize that it should not be paid for in the same way as is higher education in this country, through the charging of fees and the provision of loans.

Critics of this proposal ask how much this shift in financing remediation would cost and who would pay for it. Could the reduction in federal costs of interest subsidies and defaults resulting from less borrowing be used to offset the higher costs to institutions of not charging tuition for remedial courses? How would the rest of this loss in revenue to institutions be replaced? The need to replace all or most of this important institutional revenue stream should not obscure the difficult ethical questions raised by a practice that places so many poor students even more at risk. The basic answer is that states and localities—perhaps with pecuniary encouragement from the federal government—must be prepared to help finance the costs of remediation for coursework that should have been provided by the high schools.

IMPROVING THE PERFORMANCE OF STUDENTS
WHILE IN COLLEGE

A number of public and institutional policies affect the performance of low-income students once they enroll in college. The ones examined here include state funding of public institutions; the creation and expansion of access-oriented institutions; government, institutional, and private student financial aid efforts; and federal and state tax policies to help students and their families.

STATE FUNDING OF PUBLIC INSTITUTIONS. The principal form of taxpayer support for higher education in the United States is the funds that states provide to public institutions. Close to $60 billion is currently offered annually, and the principal manifestation of this support is the subsidized tuition that public institutions charge their in-state students.[24]

Although public sector tuition levels have increased at twice the rate of inflation for the past two decades, they remain a small fraction of the cost of providing that education and are a bargain relative to the large economic benefits they generate. Community colleges charged an average of $1,600 in tuition and fees in 1999–2000, state colleges and universities charged slightly in excess of $3,000, and land grant institutions charged closer to $4,000. While tuition and fees as a revenue source for public institutions have grown substantially, they still represent one-quarter or less of total revenues for public institutions, up from one-tenth as recently as the early 1980s.[25]

Low tuition has been pursued as a primary strategy for enhancing access, but the problem with this traditional funding structure is that the subsidies necessary to keep public tuition and fees low relative to costs are not targeted specifically on low-income students. With uniform tuition levels, students from all income brackets attending public institutions receive the same benefit.

Although systematic data are no longer available on the income distribution of students attending public institutions, earlier census survey data and more current periodic data collections indicate that the family income of students at public institutions exceeds the national average.[26] This is particularly true for public flagship schools, where surveys in selected states in recent years have revealed that the average incomes of students often are higher than at private institutions in the state.[27] To the extent that the income distribution of students enrolled in public institutions tends to be more tilted toward the middle class, the subsidies provided through low tuition are not progressive in nature. The traditional system of state higher education finance—relatively low fees combined with high and rising admissions standards at public flagship institutions—has contributed to a stratified pattern in which low-income students are relegated disproportionately to less prestigious institutions or find they can only enroll in open admissions institutions.

Another flaw in how states finance their higher education systems is that few make adequate provision for the inevitability of economic recessions. In each of the last three national economic recessions of the twentieth century—the mid-1970s, the early 1980s, and the early 1990s—public sector tuition increased by double-digit percentages as shortfalls in state revenues led to steeper hikes in user charges. Despite this experience, as the new century began most states found themselves unprepared for economic slowdown and started raising tuition once again. These fee increases fall disproportionately on the lowest income groups, especially if student aid funding is not increased commensurately to provide a safety net for the most disadvantaged students.

It also is the case that in virtually all states the process of funding public institutions of higher education is not well designed to encourage higher levels of preparation and performance. States as a general matter do not differentiate how much funding they provide to institutions based on the level of preparation of students at those institutions; colleges and universities receive the same amount of funds for ill-prepared students as for the best-prepared students. In addition, in most states, operational support is allocated to institutions primarily on the basis of the number of students enrolled in the fall rather than on determination of how many complete their year of study or receive a degree. And, in most states, the flagship institutions—those with the most affluent students—receive a larger per capita grant than others in the state system.

As a result, these policies in the states provide little incentive for institutions to worry about the K–12 preparation of their students or to improve patterns of persistence and degree completion because their funding is tied principally to how many students enroll in the fall. Moreover, in most states public institutions continue to receive funds for students who remain in school longer than the prescribed amount of time (four undergraduate years), with little or no financial penalty attached.

For states to become more active participants in efforts to improve the preparation and performance of low-income students, changes are needed in how most of them finance higher education. One way would be for states to offer a premium for such students in their funding formulas, paying public institutions more for the disadvantaged students they enroll and graduate than for students who come from families with higher incomes. Another important reform would be for states to base at least some of their funding of institutions on the numbers of students who graduate or complete each year of study rather than in the traditional way, based on the number of students who enroll.

ACCESS-ORIENTED INSTITUTIONS. In the remarkable expansion of participation in American higher education since the end of the Second World War, several types of institutions in particular have been relied upon to serve large numbers and proportions of low-income and minority students: community colleges, urban universities, and historically black colleges and universities (HBCUs).

There is ample evidence that these institutions have succeeded in their primary mission of increasing access. Community colleges now matriculate 5.5 million students, more than one-third of all U.S. higher education enrollments; they enroll roughly one-half of all entering students. Urban universities represent a major route to higher education for students living in the cities, representing nearly 10 percent of total enrollments in the United States.[28] HBCUs also have been a primary avenue of education opportunity for black students in this country; they now enroll more than 275,000 students—about one-quarter of all blacks engaged in four-year programs of study.[29]

It appears that these access-oriented institutions have enhanced opportunities and enroll a disproportionate share of low-income students, according to data sources that (unfortunately) date back to the 1970s.[30] In 1978, for example, one-third of dependent, unmarried students in community colleges had family incomes below $15,000 (roughly the median income at that time), compared to less than one-quarter of the students enrolled in the first or second year of four-year institutions.[31] No parallel data appear to exist for HBCUs or urban four-year institutions, but the fact that a higher proportion of their students are from ethnic/racial minority backgrounds suggests there may be a similarly substantial proportion of low-income students in attendance.

But in terms of improving the academic performance and staying power of low-income students in higher education, these access-oriented institutions appear to have done less well. In part because their mission is tied explicitly to providing access, they are likely to have a higher proportion of students who are not fully prepared to do college-level work (reflecting the inadequacies of the K–12 education system) than more selective institutions. To meet the needs of these students, access-oriented institutions are more likely to offer remedial courses. In 1999–2000, roughly three-quarters of all institutions offered remedial services to their students, but virtually all community colleges did so.[32]

Partially as a result of the relatively low levels of preparation, access-oriented institutions also have low degree completion rates when compared to other categories of institutions. Although the available statistics vary and are subject to much debate, it seems fair to say that only one-fifth of the students who initially enroll in a community college receive an associate's degree within five years and less than one-tenth ultimately receive a baccalaureate after transferring to a four-year institution.[33] This is to some extent a function of low transfer rates— only one-quarter or less of students who enroll in community colleges transfer to a four-year college or university, with or without an associate's degree.[34] While HBCUs award roughly one-third of all baccalaureate degrees received by black students, their degree completion rates nevertheless fall below the national average.[35]

It may be the case that to improve preparation and performance of the students who attend access-oriented institutions, no special set of policies needs to be adopted. That is, the proposed solutions of enhanced funding of early intervention and reforms in how remediation is financed would be sufficient.

But surely other changes are needed as well that would be designed to meet the needs of the students who attend these vital institutions. One example would be any initiative that seeks to improve the transfer rate of students who take and successfully complete associate's degrees in community colleges. A step in this direction would be for states to pay four-year institutions more for the community college students they enroll in upperclass undergraduate programs than for the students that progressed through these four-year programs from the start.

STUDENT AID. Student financial aid has been the principal federal policy supporting the attendance of low-income students in higher education since the passage of the Higher Education Act of 1965. The preeminence of the federal role in student aid grew with the enactment of Pell Grants in 1972. States have been the junior partner in the student aid effort; they now spend about one-third of what the federal government devotes to student aid and account for a much smaller percentage of all assistance when federal loan volume is included in the equation.[36] (Of course, states remain the senior partner in the overall financing structure for higher education through their support of public institutions and the consequential low tuition these institutions charge.)[37]

The search for why student aid has not been more successful in closing the participation gap and improving preparation and performance needs to extend beyond the question of who is responsible for funding to how the programs work and who receives the benefits. How have student aid programs influenced patterns of persistence and performance, and how well are they targeted?

While the aid programs are primarily designed for affordability, they lack meaningful academic requirements for students to fulfill in order to gain or maintain their aid eligibility. As discussed above, lax rules for determining student eligibility for aid contributed to the growth in the numbers of entering students who were not really prepared to do college-level work. Low levels of preparation adversely affect the likelihood that students will complete their programs and receive a degree.

The standards used to determine whether students can continue to receive aid once they enroll are suspect. The statutory language is that students must maintain "satisfactory academic progress" in order to maintain their aid eligibility. But the term "satisfactory" has never been defined in great detail, and responsibility for determining the progress of individual students has been largely left to the institutions themselves.[38]

One means for improving the preparation and performance of students thus would be to build features into the student aid programs that would promote these goals. In theory, this could be accomplished in one of several ways:

◆ restricting the "ability to benefit" provisions by reducing or eliminating eligibility for nonhigh school graduates;

◆ strengthening the "satisfactory progress" requirements already in the legislation, for example, by attaching grade point stipulations to the receipt of student aid;

◆ capping the length of time that students may receive aid, such as limiting aid to six years of coursework for students enrolled in four-year programs.

The problem with pursuing many of these possible solutions is that they could create incentives that run contrary to other important goals like improving quality or increasing access. Restricting student aid awards to those who receive a certain grade level could easily lead to grade inflation or otherwise reduced institutional quality standards, especially if the dollar benefits attached to success are high. Similarly, removing "ability to benefit" provisions would restrict access for many underprepared students who surely would gain from the educational opportunities being provided.

Given the potentially large adverse consequences of aggressive approaches that would alter the rules of student aid to promote better preparation and performance, one should be careful in advocating such policy shifts. It also may be the case that student aid is not the best vehicle for pursuing such objectives. Other policy recommendations—for example, altering state funding formulas to reward institutions that increase their graduation rates—could yield benefits in this regard as long as adequate quality controls are maintained to prevent a debasement of graduation requirements.

A key issue is whether the student aid programs are well targeted on low-income students. Gary Orfield, writing back in 1992, began with the following observation:

> A generation after the U.S. government made a massive commitment to making college education available to all, minority and low income access is declining, financial aid is going to students who could manage without it, and the middle class is finding more friends in Congress than are the poor.[39]

In the intervening decade, participation across all income groups has continued to increase, but much of what Orfield wrote still applies. The middle class is flexing its political muscle in a variety of ways when it comes to student aid, notably pressing for greater use of merit-based assistance and passage of a variety of tax-based savings incentives and provisions to offset current tuition expenses.

Pell Grants remain the best targeted of the federal student aid programs, with an estimated 90 percent of the benefits received by students with incomes less than $40,000 (although this is a bit misleading because roughly half of all student aid recipients are financially independent of their parents, and it is student income that is being reported).[40] Federal grants as a general matter are much better focused on low-income students than are loans. For dependent undergraduates with family incomes between $60,000 and $80,000 in 1995–96, less than 1 percent received a federal grant, whereas more than one-quarter of these students took out a federally sponsored loan.[41]

Perhaps as interesting, in that same survey, middle-income students participated almost equally in grant and loan programs when nonfederal aid was included: 25.3 percent of the students with family incomes between $60,000 to $80,000 received some form of grant aid, while 27.0 percent borrowed. This suggests that other forms of assistance, particularly from institutions in the form of tuition discounts, may be offsetting much of the targeting on low-income students provided through federal aid programs.

Coordinating all the student aid programs—federal and otherwise—to concentrate the benefits on low-income students, thereby improving their chances for success, will be difficult to achieve given the political pressures to use aid to enhance affordability for the middle class. But it could be achieved in a number of ways. One would be to change the eligibility rules for aid so that middle-income students would not qualify for as much aid as they do now. Another would be to discontinue using total costs of attendance in determining eligibility for aid, a step similar to the practice employed in determining Pell Grants, for which the difference in price already matters little with regard to how much students receive. The use of total costs of attendance in figuring student eligibility for federal student loans is a prime reason that many middle- and upper-income students going to high-priced institutions are able to quality for valuable interest subsidies.

TAX INCENTIVES. In the 1990s federal and state tax incentives became a much more prominent component in the American higher education financing structure. Previously the principal tax provision was the ability of parents to claim a deduction for their eighteen- to twenty-two-year-old children only if they were enrolled in college. But this changed beginning in the late 1980s, when the state of Michigan introduced a plan that allowed parents and others to invest in funds that would guarantee existing tuition levels in the future. The promoters of this plan depended on the Internal Revenue Service to issue a favorable ruling on how the buildup in these funds would be treated for tax purposes.

In the intervening years most states, spurred by a series of federal tax rulings and provisions that promote savings for college, have adopted tuition guarantee plans or a variety of college savings programs that do not entail a guarantee of future tuition levels but act more like private mutual funds. In addition, the federal government has enacted a number of college savings tax provisions of its own, including education savings accounts that are similar to the longer-standing Individual Retirement Accounts (IRAs).

The other prominent tax-based development in higher education over the past decade was the approval of tuition tax credits in 1997. One of the two resulting tax credits, HOPE (Helping Outstanding Pupils Educationally), was modeled after a scholarship program of the same name in Georgia. It provides tax credits against tuition expenses incurred during the first two years of college. The other tuition tax credit—Lifetime Learning—is intended to help individuals of whatever age whenever they enroll at any postsecondary level for as little as one course. More than half of all students are now eligible for one or the other of the tuition tax credits.[42]

The primary problem with all of these tax provisions is that they benefit mostly middle- and upper-class students whose families have the resources to save for their children's education and who reap the largest tax benefits from deductions for savings. Although both the 1997 tax credits have income limits that initially capped benefits for families with incomes in excess of $100,000, the vast bulk of the tax breaks will go to students with family incomes between $40,000 and $80,000, particularly since the credits were not made refundable to low-income families (that is, those who pay little or no tax would still get the full credit if it were refundable). And these income limits will only increase over time. The benefits of the various tax savings provisions even more heavily favor wealthier families than the tuition tax credits because there are more generous income limitations or no limits at all and because tax deductions by their nature provide higher benefits to higher-income taxpayers than tax credits as a result of the affluent being in higher tax brackets.

In respect to preparation and performance, the various tax provisions share the problem that limits the effectiveness of student aid programs: whether students or their families are able to benefit from either the tuition tax credits or tax savings incentives does not depend in any significant degree on whether they are prepared to go to college or whether they finish their program. The taxpaying family of any student who incurs tuition for an approved postsecondary education program is eligible for these tax benefits regardless of whether the student can handle the work. And the eligibility to receive benefits is not conditioned on whether they complete their program in the prescribed amount of time or whether they ever receive a degree.

One means for enhancing the capability of various tax provisions to improve the preparation and performance of low-income students is to build preparation or performance requirements, or both, into them. But tax provisions would face the same problem as the student aid programs in introducing stricter requirements. If anything, proposed changes would be even more difficult to implement since tax provisions generate very little in the way of administrative burden on institutions as things stand.

Better targeting of the various tax provisions would be even more difficult because the value of the benefit depends fundamentally on the structure of the tax code and on how much in taxes each individual is responsible for, a much broader set of issues than how people pay for college. A more practical and perhaps better solution would be to allow the various tax provisions to shoulder more of the burden of making college more affordable for the middle class, thus justifying a restructuring of the student aid programs to assist primarily low-income students.

RECOMMENDATIONS AND CONCLUSION

To improve the preparation and performance of low-income students, what is needed is an integrated approach in which federal, state, and local policies as well as institutional practices focus more on the needs of such students at each stage of the educational pipeline. To that end, the reforms in higher education policies and practices should include:

◆   Improving the academic preparation of students while in K–12 education;

◆   Strengthening the transition from high school to college;

◆   Improving the performance of students once enrolled.

IMPROVING THE PREPARATION OF STUDENTS WHILE IN HIGH SCHOOL

The problems of performance of low-income students in college start well before they are of an age to enroll in higher education. To get at the growing problem of too many students not being prepared to do college-level work, higher education institutions must increase their efforts to improve primary and secondary schooling.

ACADEMIC PARTNERSHIPS in which institutions of higher education provide assistance to K–12 schools have been a welcome development of the past two decades, but they must be different in scope and purpose if they are to become important instruments to enhance the readiness of low-income students for higher education.

1.   They must become the stated priority of institutional leadership (both administration and faculty), reinforced by leadership from the state or university system level. Substantial resources must accompany such commitments.

2. They must be focused on the needs of children from low-income backgrounds: many institutions and their schools of education do not serve large numbers or high proportions of such children in nearby communities. They must make new connections and build new programs accordingly.

3. They must be carried out on a significant scale over extended periods of time.

4. They must involve all sectors of the institution, but especially the arts and sciences faculty, in academically challenging programs.

5. They must lead to the development of strong new policy and governance arrangements for the continuing collaboration of higher education and K–12.

6. They must furnish strong incentives for the extensive involvement of higher education administrators and faculties in K–12 teaching. Too often, partnerships are labors of love for a few individuals in both institutions, in an environment where there are few extrinsic rewards—credit toward promotion and tenure, other professional advancement and esteem, or significant remuneration.

All this is to say that such partnerships must be important parts of the ongoing life of every institution of higher education, building understanding, cooperation, and support for K–12 programs that will, in turn, send forward more and better prepared students of all backgrounds, year after year.

TEACHER PREPARATION PROGRAMS must be strengthened in parallel ways—reflecting the fundamental changes in perspective that higher education must achieve:

1. They, too, must become a stated and well-supported priority of the leadership of institutions and systems of higher education.

2. They must be focused on the preparation of teachers who will educate more effectively the low-income, minority, and immigrant students who will be a steadily growing proportion of the students in K–12 and, inevitably, in higher education itself.

3.   They must involve all parts of the university in the development of stronger programs—founded on solid research about how teachers enhance the learning experience and, consequently, how teachers should best be prepared. Faculties of education and the arts and sciences must be involved collaboratively in the development of programs that train teachers to convey academic subject matter more effectively. This must be carried forward into school classroom and other clinical settings where students in teacher training and the early years of teaching itself will have extended opportunities to absorb the craft, knowledge, and perspective of their more experienced colleagues. Teacher education must be, in other words, a high-quality, evidence-based professional university curriculum rather than the subpar occupational training that has been countenanced for too long in much of higher education.

4.   They must offer incentives and rewards to elicit the widespread support and participation of both K–12 and higher education professionals and faculty.

5.   They must continue to have opportunities for research and innovation to build a sturdier knowledge base for K–12 teaching and to develop stronger training programs—activities supported by federal research programs and by Title II of the Higher Education Act.

STRENGTHENING THE TRANSITION FROM HIGH SCHOOL TO COLLEGE

A fundamental weakness of current arrangements is the lack of an effective transition from high school to college. This is especially true for low-income students, who find so many obstacles in their path. To improve their level of preparation prior to enrollment and to increase their chances of success once in college, a number of steps should be taken.

PRECOLLEGE SUPPORT SERVICES AND EARLY INTERVENTION should be funded at a higher level and modified to increase their effectiveness. Upward Bound and Talent Search, two programs designed to identify promising but poor students and provide them with necessary support services for success, were established as part of TRIO at the same time as many of the federal student aid programs in 1965. But while federal student aid is now integral to the overall financing of American higher education, all of the TRIO programs remain largely a demonstration on several hundred campuses and communities—available to some, but not most, low-income students. This disparity in emphasis and funding between student financial assistance and support services needs to be rectified if the transition from high school to college is ever to be made easier.

More recently, GEAR-UP was established in 1998 as an early intervention program to build on the successes of hundreds of small private efforts that over the past decade had adopted classes in schools with high concentrations of low-income students. Despite great enthusiasm among higher education institutions in applying for GEAR-UP funds to form school-university partnerships, there has been limited money available for this program for a variety of political and other considerations. Support must increase considerably if GEAR-UP is to become a major element of federal policy. In addition, GEAR-UP is one of the few federal programs that includes an evaluation component in the legislation. This provision should be invoked, and the results of any evaluation should be reflected in future changes to the program.

ALIGNED STANDARDS AND ADMISSIONS OF K–12 AND HIGHER EDUCATION SYSTEMS are needed if the participation and performance of low-income students in higher education are to improve. K–12 systems struggling to apply higher academic standards to all students need the reinforcement that only consistent and coordinated higher education admissions policies (and also, on closer examination, course placements) can afford. Higher education must acknowledge and take on this responsibility; federal and state requirements and incentives will be needed for this to happen. In the long run, much of this alignment will occur post hoc, through the development of "shared" academic offerings (for example, community college courses and programs like early colleges open to high school students, advanced placement courses and distance learning programs offering college credit to high school students, or jointly developed remedial programs), which will collectively become diverse pathways to further learning—ameliorating, or circumventing, in effect, the inflexibilities and unpredictabilities of current admissions and placement routines. Such developments should be vigorously pursued as experimental and demonstration programs.

REDESIGNING THE DELIVERY AND FINANCING OF REMEDIATION is vital to improving both the preparation and performance of low-income students. The growing number of students who require remediation before they enroll is one clear indicator that lack of preparation remains a chronic problem. The available evidence also indicates that students requiring remediation are disproportionately from low-income circumstances.

The great shame of the current system is that many students requiring remediation are forced to borrow to pay for learning that they should have been afforded for free in high school. Given that students requiring remediation often do not complete their education and are more likely to default on their student loan obligations, it is that much more important to limit or eliminate their need to borrow.

The most direct and effective way to tackle this problem is for institutions to stop charging tuition for the remedial courses they offer and for the federal government to not allow borrowing to cover the instructional costs, even as students should remain eligible for grant assistance to cover living costs. This solution would require some combination of states, localities, and the federal government to help finance the costs of remediation on the premise that students ought to have received basic skills while enrolled in K–12 education.

IMPROVING THE PERFORMANCE OF LOW-INCOME STUDENTS WHILE ENROLLED IN COLLEGE

Of the three phases of education discussed in this report, improving the performance of students once they enroll is probably the most neglected in terms of federal and state policies. Student aid policies are notorious for their lack of emphasis on performance, and support services typically fall off once students enroll in a higher education program. Problems for low-income students just accumulate as they make their way through the educational process. To remedy the problem of poor performance among low-income students, several policy initiatives at the federal and state levels are important.

PROVIDING SUSTAINED MENTORING AND SUPPORT SERVICES once low-income students are enrolled represents an important component in the effort to bolster their performance. Evaluations of precollege public initiatives such as Upward Bound as well as privately funded ventures suggest that gains made before college often are dissipated through a lack of follow-up mentoring and support once students hit the campus. This has led many private sponsors to seek assurances that progress will be maintained by institutions.

It is similarly essential that publicly funded programs such as the Special Services components of TRIO at the federal level and the many state and locally funded offerings of support services be available to all low-income students. Program design also is important so that students who participate in precollege programs are tracked through higher education and their performance evaluated.

BETTER TARGETING OF STUDENT AID PROGRAMS is a critical component of any effort to improve the participation and performance of low-income students as well as increasing their participation, which remains the programs' primary goal. Lost in most of the debates over federal student aid is the fact that such federal programs are not that well targeted. Political pressures to extend benefits up the income scale as college tuition and other charges have exploded help to explain the relative neglect of the poor in federal and state student aid programs.

The largest federal student aid program—Pell Grants—is reasonably well targeted on low-income students because the aid formula has more to do with family circumstances than overall college expenses. But all of the other federal aid programs use total costs of attendance in defining financial need, with the result that many middle-class students qualify for aid, especially if they attend high-priced institutions. At the state level, there has been a shift toward merit-based aid programs that also tend to expand eligibility for aid to the middle class.

If student aid programs are to become more effective in helping the poor, it will be important for federal and state policymakers to resist the political pressures continually to expand middle-class benefits. The creation of tuition tax credits and savings incentives in recent years to aid middle-class students and nontraditional learners actually could help in this regard if their growing availability could be used as a rationale for allowing student aid programs to concentrate more on students whose families earn too little to benefit much from tax-based benefits in any form.

More controversially, government student aid programs and institutional financial aid and discount policies could be redesigned to provide incentives and stipulations to prod students to reach for higher achievement and to stay in school until completion of a degree program. Such measures might feature restricting aid eligibility based on "ability to benefit" provisions, cutting off aid benefits if students

exceed some stated length of time to degree fulfillment (say, six years
for a four-year program), or requiring real academic standards for
students to maintain their eligibility for aid rather than the bland and
largely unenforced concept of "satisfactory academic progress." Such
proposals, however, would be especially difficult to design so as to
avoid adverse effects on low-income students.

MODIFYING STATE FUNDING FORMULAS to reward institutions for enrolling
and graduating low-income students would represent an important
step in the effort to improve both participation and performance. While
the discussion of the plight of these students in higher education typically and rightly focuses on demand-side issues such as augmenting
student financial aid, it also is important to explore how the number of
seats supplied by institutions for them might be increased.

Most states utilize funding formulas that pay institutions on the
basis of the number who nenroll in the fall with no mind toward
whether those students complete the year's study or their degree. In
addition, few states make any distinction within their funding formulas for students who come from disadvantaged circumstances.

States should reconsider these funding policies in order to complement any measures taken on the demand side, offering students
incentives to perform well and earn their degrees. In addition, paying
institutions more for the disadvantaged youth they enroll or, better
yet, graduate could prove to be a powerful supply-side incentive for
colleges and universities to focus more carefully on the needs and
achievement of such students.

~

Looking at all these programs and policies together, it is evident that
higher education, as a policy system or as a universe of individual
campuses, lacks a consistent, effective focus on those coming from
low-income backgrounds—one that acknowledges, anticipates, and
addresses the range of challenges that face them. Once access has been
granted to these students, the approach of higher education toward
them seems to be mostly remedial and compensatory in character,
resembling primary and secondary school policies a quarter century
ago. The key question for future success is whether higher education
can make the transformation that K–12 education has made to hold
itself to high standards and performance for all students.

3

SOCIOECONOMIC STATUS, RACE/ETHNICITY, AND SELECTIVE COLLEGE ADMISSIONS

Anthony P. Carnevale and Stephen J. Rose

The issue of affirmative action at our nation's top universities excites much interest and controversy in part because it goes to the very heart of what Americans mean by equal opportunity and meritocracy. Race-conscious admissions received an important boost with the Supreme Court's recent decision affirming the constitutionality of the University of Michigan Law School's program—an outcome we support. This chapter seeks to expand the traditional debate over race and ethnicity in selective admissions by analyzing the issue of whether low-income students, too, should benefit from affirmative action policies.

Along the way, it asks a series of questions: Who attends selective universities today? Does it matter who gets in? How do college administrators define merit and fairness in the admissions process? How are they defined by the public? How should they be defined? Do colleges currently give a leg up to economically disadvantaged students? If not, would students admitted under such preferences be qualified to do rigorous, college-level work? What would be the effect of replacing affirmative action with a variety of policies: a straight system of grades and test scores; a lottery of minimally qualified students; automatic admissions to the top-ranking students in all high schools, irrespective of standardized test scores; an automatic admissions plan for top-ranking students with a minimum standardized test score requirement; preferences for economically disadvantaged students?

If economic preferences are advisable, should they replace or supplement racial affirmative action?

To answer these questions, we analyzed information from two sets of longitudinal data published by the National Center for Education Statistics (NCES). These data sets are extremely detailed, with individualized records of high school grades, college entrance exams, and socioeconomic background. Each student monitored also took a test that provides a wealth of information about the many students who do not take the Scholastic Assessment Test (SAT) or American College Test (ACT). We also analyze data on how admissions officers currently make decisions as well as trends in admissions decisions between 1979 and 2000, and we relay the findings of an Educational Testing Service (ETS) poll of the American public on admissions questions. We then apply these data to the nation's most competitive 146 four-year colleges, which constitute the top two tiers in Barron's guide to colleges (those that are among the most selective 10 percent of approximately fourteen hundred four-year institutions and 6 percent of all postsecondary institutions).

The next part of this chapter finds that, under current affirmative action policies, racial minorities are underrepresented and that the underrepresentation of low-income students is even greater. The chapter then looks at the three main advantages of attending a selective institution: greater likelihood of graduating, greater access to graduate schooling, and a wage premium in the labor market. The chapter goes on to examine the evidence surrounding how merit is defined by different audiences and concludes that a dynamic concept of merit, which looks at how far someone has traveled as well as where he or she ends up, is widely accepted as appropriate. We find that preferences for minority status and the economically disadvantaged have fallen off over the past thirty years. We then note that while selective colleges purport to provide preferences to low-income students and say they would like to admit more if these students were academically prepared, on average the top 146 colleges do not provide a systemic preference and could in fact admit far greater numbers of low-income students, including minority students, capable of handling the work. The chapter then simulates the effects of a variety of race-neutral admissions schemes, reaching, among others, the following conclusions: a system of grades and test scores would significantly reduce racial and ethnic diversity but would increase income diversity slightly; lottery admissions have little public support; class rank plans without a minimum test score would greatly raise dropout rates; class rank plans with a minimum test score would reduce racial and ethnic diversity; economic preferences would somewhat diminish racial and ethnic diversity and greatly expand socioeconomic diversity.

In the final section of this chapter, we make a series of policy recommendations, cautioning against the widespread use of the class rank approach to admissions because doing so can force a trade-off between diversity and attainment of a degree. We urge the expansion of current affirmative action programs to include low-income students because these add both economic and racial diversity. Maintaining existing racial affirmative action schemes is paramount in the interest of racial justice and the educational benefits of diversity. And stronger financial aid policies must be implemented to make offers of admissions to low-income students genuine rather than hollow commitments.

Study Design

To demonstrate the complex reality of college admissions, this chapter examines the academic characteristics of students who attend institutions at every level of selectivity (see Box 3.1, page 104, for treatment of the Barron's definition of competitive colleges). It analyzes this information based on two sets of longitudinal data published by the National Center for Education Statistics: the National Education Longitudinal Study of 1988 (hereafter referred to as NELS:88) and the High School and Beyond study (to be referred to as HS&B).

Approximately 1.2 million high school students who graduate each year enroll in one of the fourteen hundred accredited four-year colleges. Few of these students (15 percent) will make it into a top-tier four-year college. Another 20 percent will matriculate in a second-tier school. The largest population (about 40 percent) enroll in third-tier institutions, with the remaining 25 percent going to fourth-tier colleges. So the top two tiers account for slightly more than one-third of enrollees.

The NELS:88 study began by collecting data on approximately twenty-five thousand high school freshmen in 1988 and followed them through graduation in 1992 and their post-high school years to 1994. The HS&B study began in 1980 and continued to collect information on approximately thirty thousand respondents during their college years and their first jobs.

BOX 3.1 BARRON'S DEFINITION OF COMPETITIVE COLLEGES

The Barron's selectivity measures take into account several determinants: the median SAT I or median composite ACT entrance exam score; students' high school class rank; students' grade point average; and the percentage of students accepted.

The Barron's selectivity measures group schools into six different levels from the most selective to the least selective: *Most Competitive, Highly Competitive, Very Competitive, Competitive, Less Competitive*, and *Noncompetitive*.

This chapter uses a simplified version that condenses the six levels into four tiers.

TOP TIER "Most" and "Highly" Competitive. Generally, students in this tier are in the top 35 percent of their high school class, have a high school grade point average that is B or better, and score about 1240 on the SAT I or above 27 on the ACT. Colleges in this tier accept less than 50 percent of the applicants. There are 146 four-year colleges in this category, and approximately 170,000 students enroll as freshmen at these institutions each year.

Only a tiny percentage of the student population applies to the 146 most selective colleges, a few hundred thousand out of three million high school graduates each year, and an even smaller group attends. Enrollments at the most selective 146 colleges represent less than 10 percent of the nation's post-secondary freshman class, including four- and two-year colleges.

SECOND TIER "Very" Competitive. Colleges in this tier accept students in the middle of their class who have a high school grade point average of B- or higher and a range of 1146–1238 on the SAT I or 24–26 on the ACT. The applicant acceptance rate is between 50 and 75 percent. Approximately three hundred thousand freshmen attend the 253 four-year colleges in this category.

THIRD TIER "Competitive." Colleges in this tier generally accept students with a minimum high school grade point average of C, those who score above 1000 on the SAT I or above 21 on the ACT. The "preferred" students are in the top 50 to 65 percent of their high school class. Colleges in Barron's third tier generally accept 75–85 percent of their applicants. The 588 four-year institutions in this category enroll 570,000 freshmen.

FOURTH TIER "Less" Competitive and "Noncompetitive." These colleges accept students with scores below 1000 on the SAT I or below 21 on the ACT. The minimum grade point average is C or less and high school rank is in the top 65 percent. College acceptance rate generally exceeds 85 percent. These 429 institutions generally enroll about 325,000 freshmen annually.

Source: Barron's: Profiles of American Colleges, 24th ed. (Hauppauge, N.Y.: Barron's Educational Series, Inc., 2000).

Both the HS&B and NELS:88 surveys were remarkably detailed. A complete record of high school and college courses taken, as well as grades and college entrance exam scores, was created for each participant. In addition, each student, along with his or her parents, teachers, and principal, answered a wide range of questions about expectations, practices in the home and in the classroom, the student's academic progress, high school environment, and so forth. Finally, each student was given a National Education Longitudinal Survey (NELS) test, an exam similar to the SAT. Since not all students take a college entrance exam, the NELS test provides a good benchmark for all students.

In determining family background, both HS&B and NELS:88 computed a measure of the socioeconomic status of the family on the basis of reported income and parental education and occupations. Clifford Adelman recommends using socioeconomic status because family income is most often reported by the student and prone to large mistakes.[1]

Each student record is unique: what high school he or she attended; which courses he or she took; his or her overall grade point average, extracurricular activities, and teacher recommendations. Because there is variation among high school grading practices and courses taken, college entrance exam and NELS test scores are used to facilitate comparisons across schools and curricula. For this reason, exam scores are often used as the best available single statistic describing student achievement.[2]

High school grades and class rank correlate with college entrance exam scores but not completely. For example, even among students in the top 10 percent of their high school class, 24 percent either did not take the SAT or ACT or scored below 1000 on their combined math and English tests, while 43 percent had scores topping 1300.

WHO ATTENDS SELECTIVE UNIVERSITIES

Access to selective colleges is highly skewed by race and ethnicity, although not as much as by socioeconomic status. While Asians attain a greater share of seats in four-year colleges than their proportion of the population of eighteen-year-olds, African Americans and Hispanics constituted only 6 percent each of the freshman classes of the 146 "most" and "highly" selective four-year colleges. African Americans and Hispanics were 15 and 13 percent, respectively, of all eighteen-year-olds in 1995. So blacks and Hispanics were considerably under-represented at these top schools even with affirmative action.

There is even less socioeconomic diversity than racial or ethnic diversity at the most selective colleges (see Table 3.1). Seventy-four percent of the students at the top 146 highly selective colleges came from families in the top quarter of the socioeconomic status scale (as measured by combining family income and the education and occu-pations of the parents), just 3 percent came from the bottom socio-economic status quartile, and roughly 10 percent came from the bottom half of the socioeconomic status scale.[3]

If attendance at these institutions reflected the population at large, 85,000 students (rather than 17,000) would have been from the bot-tom two socioeconomic status quartiles. Overall, a little more than 22 percent of the students in the top tier of college selectivity are Asian, African American, or Hispanic (11 percent Asian, 6 percent black, and 6 percent Hispanic), while only 3 percent are from families in the lowest socioeconomic status quartile and only 10 percent are from

TABLE 3.1 SOCIOECONOMIC STATUS OF ENTERING CLASSES

	SES Quartiles (percentage)				
	First	Second	Third	Fourth	Total
Tier 1	3	6	17	74	100
Tier 2	7	18	29	46	100
Tier 3	10	19	36	35	100
Tier 4	16	21	28	35	100
Community Colleges	21	30	27	22	100

Source: Authors' analysis of the National Education Longitudinal Study of 1988 (NELS:88), National Center for Education Statistics, Washington, D.C., 1988 and subsequent years.

the bottom half of the socioeconomic status distribution. There are thus four times as many African American and Hispanic students as there are students from the lowest socioeconomic status quartile.

WHY IT MATTERS WHO ATTENDS SELECTIVE UNIVERSITIES

The economic benefits of attending a selective college are clear. Selective colleges spend as much as four times more per student and subsidize student spending by as much as $24,000, compared to a student subsidy of as little as $2,000 at the least selective colleges. Students at selective colleges have higher graduation rates than similarly qualified students at less selective colleges. In addition, the student support, preparation, and prestige at selective colleges result in higher rates of acceptance at graduate and professional schools among students who appeared comparably qualified to others coming out of high school. While the differences in earnings for equally qualified students from "less" and "more" selective schools are small, they do exist and may be understated owing to data limitations. Moreover, these differential effects are magnified for less privileged or minority students who would not have been otherwise admitted without outreach, special consideration, or support.

GRADUATION RATES

One of the major benefits of attending a top-tier college is higher graduation rates: 86 percent of students who initially enrolled in the 146 top-tier colleges ended up with bachelor's degrees. By contrast, moving down the tiers of selectivity, the graduation rates fall to 71, 61, and 54 percent, respectively (see Table 3.2, page 108)[4]. Obviously, a lot of this difference has to do with the quality of students in each tier. Table 3.2 also shows that students who have the highest SAT scores have higher graduation rates.[5]

But even adjusting for student test scores, students at top-tier colleges are more likely to complete their degree than students in the fourth-tier colleges with similar college entrance exam scores. Among students who score above 1200 on the SAT/ACT, 96 percent graduate from top-tier institutions, 86 percent graduate from second-tier colleges, and 75 percent graduate from third- and fourth-tier colleges. For those with an SAT-equivalent score between 1000 and 1100, 86 percent graduate from top-tier colleges, 83 percent from second-tier institutions, 71 percent from third-tier colleges, and only 67 percent from fourth-tier colleges.[6]

It is hard to determine empirically why the top-tier colleges have higher graduation rates than less selective colleges. Intuitively, one might expect the opposite—it would be harder to graduate from more demanding institutions. In particular, one would expect that highly talented students would have no difficulty finishing programs at less demanding institutions. But the evidence does not support either of these commonsense views. Perhaps peer interactions and high expectations about performance at top-tier colleges create an atmosphere in which students work harder and graduate. Perhaps when an institution expects everyone to graduate it is more likely to identify students having problems and to intervene to help them. Perhaps students with high expectations are drawn to colleges with matching expectations.

Table 3.3 presents the unadjusted graduation rates of students who enrolled in four-year colleges by the socioeconomic status of their family while in high school and by the selectivity of the college. While those from families in the lowest socioeconomic status quartile had a graduation rate of 55 percent, those from the highest socioeconomic status quartile had a much higher rate, 73 percent. Virtually all of this

TABLE 3.2 COLLEGE GRADUATION RATES RELATE BOTH TO
STUDENTS' SAT-EQUIVALENT SCORES AND TO
COLLEGE SELECTIVITY (PERCENTAGE)

	All	Non–Test Taker	<900	900–1000	1000–1100	1100–1200	1200–1300	>1300
All	65	58	43	69	74	74	85	88
Tier 1	86	83	30	61	86	85	96	96
Tier 2	71	65	44	71	83	70	85	90
Tier 3	61	55	45	74	71	68	78	78
Tier 4	54	45	39	61	67	83	78	68

Source: Authors' analysis of the High School and Beyond (HS&B) survey, National Center for Education Statistics, Washington, D.C., 1987 and subsequent years.

eighteen percentage point difference is determined by circumstances prior to enrolling in college—SAT scores, high school grades, rigor of high school courses taken, and the like. But the numbers in this table show that, within colleges, students from lower socioeconomic status families are more likely to have trouble graduating. At the top-tier institutions, 90 percent of students from the highest socioeconomic status quartile families graduated, while only 76 percent of those from the lowest socioeconomic status quartile graduated.

These findings are consistent with another study using HS&B in which students from low socioeconomic status families were shown to have lower college graduation rates than students from higher socioeconomic status families, even when they both had taken a rigorous high school curriculum. In this study, among those who took the same challenging coursework, more than 85 percent of high school students from families in the highest socioeconomic status quintile completed a bachelor's degree, compared with 62 percent of students from the lowest socioeconomic status quintile.[7]

POSTGRADUATE ACCESS

Another benefit of top-tier colleges is that they provide greater access to postgraduate studies. Nationally, 21 percent of those who

TABLE 3.3 COLLEGE GRADUATION RATES RELATE BOTH TO STUDENTS' SAT-EQUIVALENT SCORES AND TO COLLEGE SELECTIVITY (PERCENTAGE)

| | SES Quartiles | | | | |
	All	First	Second	Third	Fourth
All	65	55	63	63	73
Tier 1	86	76	85	80	90
Tier 2	71	61	63	71	79
Tier 3	61	60	58	59	66
Tier 4	54	40	63	55	58

Source: Authors' analysis of the High School and Beyond (HS&B) survey, National Center for Education Statistics, Washington, D.C., 1987 and subsequent years.

attend four-year colleges proceed to graduate school (see Table 3.4). However, more than 35 percent of students at the 146 top-tier colleges go on to graduate work. Moving down the scale of selectivity, the ratio of students going on progressively falls from less than 25 percent for students from second-tier colleges to 15 percent for those at third- and fourth-tier institutions.

Much of this difference is associated with differences in SAT-equivalent scores, which are strongly correlated with graduate school attendance. While relatively few who had SAT-equivalent scores below 1000 pursued a graduate education, fully 38 percent of those who scored above 1200 did so. Even holding constant the tier of college selectivity, students with higher SAT scores were more likely to pursue postbaccalaureate work. For example, in top-tier colleges, nearly half went on to graduate school if their SAT-equivalent scores were above 1200, while only one-quarter went on if their scores were between 1000 and 1200. The few students with scores below 1000 at these institutions had an even lower frequency of graduate school participation.

There is a similar interaction between SAT-equivalent score and graduate school pursuit at all levels of selectivity.[8] For second-tier colleges, those with scores above 1200 are quite likely to attend graduate school (43 percent), while only half of that number (22 percent) go on if their scores were between 1000 and 1200. For third-tier colleges, there is a clear gradient, with 28 percent headed to graduate school if their scores were above 1200 and only slightly more than 10

TABLE 3.4 GRADUATE SCHOOL ATTENDANCE BY
SAT-EQUIVALENT SCORE AND SELECTIVITY OF THE COLLEGE
(PERCENTAGE OF INITIAL ATTENDEES)

	All	<900	900–1000	1000–1200	>1200
All	21	10	13	21	38
BY LEVEL OF SELECTIVITY:					
Tier 1	35	19	15	25	48
Tier 2	25	15	14	22	43
Tier 3	18	10	15	20	28
Tier 4	15	8	9	22	26

Source: Authors' analysis of the HS&B sophomore cohort.

percent going if their scores fell below 900. At the fourth-tier colleges, an SAT-equivalent score of 1000 seems to be the dividing line: above that score, almost one in four go on to graduate work, while below that score less than one in ten do so.

In terms of going on to graduate school, the level of selectivity of colleges has a positive effect on students with similar SAT scores.[9] For example, among those with SAT-equivalent scores greater than 1200, the group most likely to attend graduate school, 48 percent of those attending top-tier colleges and 43 percent of those attending second-tier colleges pursued graduate work. However, students who scored better than 1200 but attended one of the colleges in the bottom two tiers of selectivity were much less inclined to attend graduate school. For students with scores below 1200 a similar effect is evident, although it is of a smaller magnitude.

WAGE PREMIUM

One would expect that another benefit that comes with attending a top-tier college would be greater labor market success. The research on this question is somewhat ambiguous, with the added effect of attending a highly selective college among similarly qualified students usually found to be between 5 and 20 percent. The key word here is "added." Because the top-tier colleges tend to have the highest share of talented students, it may be that it is not the institution but the student that matters most. Therefore, researchers have to look at the fate of students with similar abilities who go to colleges of differing quality.

This requirement makes getting a reliable estimate difficult. In order to perform these calculations, researchers need information about students' family backgrounds, their academic ability (grades in high school and college and college entrance exam scores), educational attainment, college major (which turns out to be important), and measures of labor force performance. The HS&B survey and a few other data sources have this information but suffer from two important weaknesses.

First, because of data limitations, estimates of earnings differences are almost always based on earnings at the beginning of careers. There are reasons to believe, however, that early earnings differences may not adequately reflect what develops later in life. For example, Robert G. Wood, Mary E. Corcoran, and Paul N. Courant compared the earnings of male and female graduates from the University of Michigan Law School (classes of 1972 through 1975). The mean first-year earnings of employed women were just 10 percent less than that of employed men, $36,850 as compared to $39,428 (in 1989 dollars). By the fifteenth year after graduation, the difference had risen to 40 percent ($86,335 to $140,917).[10] Similarly, Rachel Dunifon and Greg J. Duncan found that the effect of motivation on labor market performance was very different early in one's life than in mid-career. Using the University of Michigan's Panel Study of Income Dynamics, a longitudinal survey, they were able to perform calculations on the same men at various points in their work histories. When they were twenty-one to twenty-nine years old, the results of a psychological test meant to measure motivation showed it had no effect on earnings. But when these computations were rerun with the earnings of the same men fifteen to twenty-five years later, a positive economic impact was found for those who scored high on the motivation test administered in their twenties.[11]

Second, the available data lack adequate differentiation in critical variables. When all the students who go to selective colleges are academically able, it is difficult to separate out the effects of the college from the aptitude of the students. The ideal experiment would be to track the experience of four top students at one of the nation's best high schools, say, New Trier High in Chicago's northern suburbs, who all come from wealthy families with highly educated parents. If each of these students had identical high grades and high test scores, one could assign them to colleges that vary widely in selectivity. For statistical purposes, the best scenario would be if they all majored in the same subject. Then, if their future earnings information were to be collected, one would have a fairly reliable sense of the independent effect of the quality of the college in question.

In reality, however, all four of these top students would attend one of the top-tier colleges or a close substitute, which would provide little basis to test for the independent effect of college quality. In a series of papers, John Cawley, Jane Heckman, and Edward Vytlacil show that this lack of variation in the data may affect the results greatly.[12] So, the education policy community is left with a series of studies that may be of questionable validity.

A recent NCES publication typifies the problem of assessing earnings returns to college education measured by the selectivity of the school when the data only track students early in their careers.[13] The NCES study used HS&B data to measure the added earnings attributable to a degree from a highly selective institution five years after graduation. They tried a variety of approaches and mostly found small additional returns (about 5 to 10 percent per year) to attending a highly selective college once the original endowment of the students was taken into account. However, the same report found that there were no economic returns to attending graduate school. This is quite a surprising finding given that, among older workers, those with graduate degrees earn 30 percent more per year than those with just bachelor's degrees.[14]

Using HS&B, Thomas J. Kane found that a tightening in college selectivity, equivalent to an institution's requiring an extra 100 points on the combined SAT score for admission, resulted in a 6 percent jump in earnings. Thus, going from an average four-year college to one in the top 10 percent would tend to increase earnings by a little more than 11 percent.[15] Kermit Daniel and colleagues (using yet another survey—the 1979 National Longitudinal Survey of Youth) actually found smaller returns to college quality, with the earnings of someone attending a college in the top fifth in terms of selectivity amounting to 13 percent more than those of a person of similar characteristics who attended a college in the bottom fifth.[16]

Stacy Berg Dale and Alan B. Krueger use a highly sophisticated statistical estimation procedure on two data sets to determine whether there are substantial earnings gains from attending a more selective college.[17] They find that if colleges are ranked along Barron's scale, going to a more selective college can mean a 10 percent increase per year in one's earnings after adjusting for the quality of the student when he or she enrolls in college. However, if colleges are ranked by the SAT scores of their incoming students, no effect is found. In all cases, they find that students from low socioeconomic status families earn more than similarly situated students who do not attend highly selective colleges and get a bigger payoff than students from better-off families for going to a highly selective school.

Dominic J. Brewer, Eric Eide, and Ronald G. Ehrenberg grouped four-year colleges and universities into one of six mutually exclusive categories based upon Barron's ratings: top, middle, and less selective private colleges and top, middle, and less selective public colleges.[18] They found that, all other things being equal, there was about a 20 percent wage premium to attending initially a top private college and a 10 percent wage premium to attending a middle private college, relative to the wages earned by those initially attending a less selective public college.

Finally, Jere R. Behrman, Mark R. Rosenzweig, and Paul Taubman found much larger differences using a data source that followed 708 female pairs of twins. Each twin pair attended the same primary and secondary schools, and thus the precollege resources devoted to each twin were very similar. About half of the twins who attended college went to different institutions. This group seemingly presents a natural experiment in which most characteristics are similar or identical, with the only difference being the quality of the college attended. The designers of the study attempted to capture "college quality" through six attributes: total spending per student, size of enrollment, whether a public or private institution, students per faculty, whether the college grants Ph.D.s, and the professors' pay.

Using these criteria, they found that the twins who attended Ph.D.-granting private colleges with small enrollments and well-paid professors had significantly higher earnings later on in life. They vividly summarized the implications of these results by showing the estimated earnings differentials attributable to the distinct characteristics of four types of institutions: a large public college, a large public research university, a small private college, and a large private research university. A baccalaureate degree holder from a large public research university would earn about 32 percent more annually than if she had not gone any further than high school. If, however, she had attended a large private research university, the baccalaureate/high school earnings differential would be greater than 55 percent. Of course, tuition at a large private research university exceeds tuition at a similiar public university. Behrman and colleagues calculate that the earnings premium accruing to the possessor of a large private research university baccalaureate, as opposed to a public one, amounts to more than $170,000 (in 1994 dollars) over the person's remaining work life.[19] This suggests that attendance at private research universities may be a wise financial course, the higher expenses nothwithstanding.

All of this research seems to find that the added earnings power of attending a highly selective college is worth the extra tuition but not by orders of magnitude more than attending a less selective college. This conclusion may surprise many parents who think that the particular college their children attend is of paramount economic importance. The competition to get into the top colleges, most likely more intense than the rewards would justify, plausibly motivates students to take their coursework seriously and to try to improve their overall skill levels. Even were they aware of the relatively small payoff for bachelor's degrees at top-tier colleges, parents still might prefer sending their children to these campuses because of the peer effects of being with highly motivated and skilled students and because of the higher graduation rates and probability of continuing on to graduate school.

DEFINING MERIT AND FAIRNESS IN COLLEGE ADMISSIONS

Defining merit and fairness in admissions goes directly to the question of values. This section examines the views of admissions officers and the public, both of which define merit not just in absolute terms but also in terms of disadvantages overcome. It then presents data on how obstacles might be defined, by socioeconomic status and race.

ADMISSIONS OFFICERS

There is broad agreement among admissions officers that admission should be based on "merit." Definitions of merit vary, but the common approach of merit-based admissions decisions is to judge applicants on the basis of their high school achievements. From this perspective, students are sorted most commonly on the basis of their ranking in a hierarchy composed of grades, test scores, recommendations, leadership, and other achievements, regardless of where those achievements occurred or of the applicant's socioeconomic background. At the same time, many college officials also believe that merit is a "dynamic concept" in that it should be measured not only by the applicants' academic achievements but by how many obstacles they had to surmount to achieve them.

According to a report on admissions policy from a group of college officials convened by the College Board

> we should consider what a student has had to overcome in order to qualify for a competitive selection process. Not all students have had the same educational opportunities. For some students, even surpassing the basic eligibility hurdle in order to be considered

for admission at a selective institution represents a major achievement. . . . Contrary to the perception of some in the general public, employing an applicant's ability to overcome educational
obstacles as a selection criterion is not simply a means to correct
past inequities. . . . Students who demonstrate the ability to rise
above their early lives' social and economic limitations are likely
to face future hurdles with the same determination and perseverance.[20]

At the 1999 College Board meetings, the attendees identified nine
mission-related perspectives, many of which apply at different stages
of the admissions process and to different segments of the applicant
pool (see Box 3.2).

Two of these (entitlement and open access) are "nonselective"
in that judgments about admissions are made on the basis of general
principles rather than on a competition among students based on
their qualifications. The other seven perspectives can be thought of as
"selective" models: students are compared to each other on the basis
of certain criteria and a decision is made to admit some while not
admitting others.

Two perspectives (meritocracy and character) relate to a prospective student's capacity to perform in the college environment based on
demonstrated performance prior to college. These tend to see admission to higher education as a reward for performance in high school.

The next perspective (enhancement) places a higher value on
what the student gets out of college and conceives of higher education
as a way to bring the greatest benefit to those selected for admission.

Admissions officers also see college as a social tool to promote
upward mobility (mobilization) and to ensure that postsecondary
education does not become a passive participant in reproducing social,
cultural, and economic elites. One perspective (investment) tends to
focus on long-term social goals.

Finally, there are two perspectives (environmental/institutional and
fiduciary) concerned with the effect that potential students will have on
helping the college meet its own institutional and financial needs.

Colleges and universities also admit students to meet student
body needs, according to the College Board, "not because they are the
best candidates but because they best fit the needs of the instructional environment." Most higher education institutions feel that diversity
is essential to educational quality.

Box 3.2 The College Board Taxonomy of the Admissions Decisionmaking Process

* ENTITLEMENT
  Higher education is an inalienable right and should be made available to everyone.

* OPEN ACCESS
  College is a natural progression after high school and should be made available to everyone who is qualified.

* MERITOCRACY
  Access to higher education is a reward for those who have been most academically successful.

* CHARACTER
  Access to higher education is a reward for personal virtue, dedication, perseverance, community service, and hard work.

* ENHANCEMENT
  The goal of higher education is to seek out and nurture talent.

* MOBILIZATION
  Higher education is the "great equalizer" and must promote social and economic mobility.

* INVESTMENT
  Access to higher education should promote the greater good and further the development of society.

* ENVIRONMENTAL/INSTITUTIONAL
  The admissions selection process is designed to meet the enrollment goals and unique organizational needs of the admitting institution while promoting the overall quality of students' educational experience.

* FIDUCIARY
  Higher education is a business, and access must first preserve the institution's fiscal integrity.

Source: Adapted from Greg A. Perfetto, "Toward a Taxonomy of the Admissions Decision-Making Process," College Board, New York, 1999.

At the same time, virtually all colleges and universities devise admissions policies intended to achieve broad social goals. These goals are most often associated with promoting broadly based inclusion not only in higher education but in society itself. In some cases, postsecondary institutions attempt to make up for inequality in the opportunity to learn in the K–12 education system, or they choose students who seem likely to make significant contributions to the community at large or to its minority or low socioeconomic status components. This viewpoint suggests that institutions need to look beyond standardized measures of achievement to consider how students might excel if given a chance.

The view that students ought to be selected based on their ability to benefit or their ability to contribute in the broader society turns the traditional admissions model on its head. It focuses on the enrichment the college gives to the student rather than the value added by the student to the institution.

The best available data on trends in student application and college admissions decisions come from four surveys of college admissions practices conducted by various professional societies and testing agencies in 1979, 1985, 1992, and 2000. A joint effort among survey sponsors to track the longitudinal implications of those separate inquiries was finished in 2000.[21] The figures used in the following paragraphs are based on their hard work.

Over the 1992 to 2000 period, the share of colleges that actively recruited minority students fell from 67 to 51 percent. The largest falloff was in public colleges, where the anti–affirmative action movement has had its strongest impact. Minority recruitment declined from 91 to 66 percent of four-year public colleges and from 66 to 49 percent of two-year public colleges. The share of private colleges involved in minority recruitment also declined, from 65 to 54 percent in four-year private colleges and from 36 to 21 percent in two-year private colleges (see Table 3.5).

The number of colleges that recruit economically disadvantaged students is generally a little more than half of those that recruit minorities. The percentage actively enouraging applications from economically disadvantaged students remained the same in four-year private colleges (24 percent) and declined in two-year private colleges (from 24 to 16 percent). Among public institutions, the shares of institutions that recruited such high schoolers increased slightly for two-year public colleges (from 45 to 47 percent) and dropped from 44 to 37 percent in four-year public colleges.

TABLE 3.5 SPECIAL RECRUITING ACTIVITIES
TARGETING SUBGROUPS OF STUDENTS, 1992 AND 2000 (PERCENTAGE)

Group	Two-Year Public		Two-Year Private		Four-Year Public		Four-Year Private		All Institutions	
	1992	2000	1992	2000	1992	2000	1992	2000	1992	2000
Racial/ethnic minorities	66	49	36	21	91	66	65	54	67	51
Disadvantaged	45	47	24	16	44	37	24	24	35	33
Students with disabilities	35	31	15	12	21	12	12	10	22	17
Students with special talents in art, music, etc.	36	33	30	18	71	54	59	57	51	46
Adults seeking career change	65	63	63	58	59	43	55	41	60	52
Adults improving technical skills	*	62	*	50	*	*	*	*	*	*
Adults maintaining currency in job	*	60	*	46	*	*	*	*	*	*
Out of state/district	28	31	40	31	55	57	59	52	46	45
Part-time students	45	48	40	33	25	21	29	21	35	32
Veterans	32	27	29	28	24	15	13	8	23	17
Institutions responding to questionnaire	705	505	169	177	366	305	784	657	2,024	1,644

Notes: 2000 summary data for this table were obtained from responses to questions 18 and 30 of the two- and four-year questionnaires, respectively. Percentages are based on the total number of institutions responding to the questionnaire.

*Not included in the questionnaire for fall 1992 for two-year institutions or in four-year questionnaire.

Source: Hunter Breland et al., *Trends in College Admission 2000: A Report of a Survey of Undergraduate Admissions Policies, Practices, and Procedures,* sponsored by ACT, Inc., Association for Institutional Research, College Board, Edcational Testing Service, and National Association for College Admission Counseling, 2000.

Trends in financial aid practices in colleges between 1979 and 2000 did not favor low-income and minority students. More than 80 percent of all institutions continued admitting students before aid is considered, a practice that creates "sticker price shock" and discourages low-income student applications. In all postsecondary institutions except two-year public colleges, there was an increase in the percentage of students whose financial needs were not fully met between 1992 and 2000, a finding consistent with other data. Survey respondents also reported an increase in the average amount of unmet need. Although the share of colleges that give aid to minority and low-income students is rising, aid for academically talented students is more pervasive (see Table 3.6). The share of state aid going to students whose families are not in need of assistance is rising. Respondents in the 2000 survey estimated an average increase of 36 percent in "no need" awards since 1995. Financial aid for the economically disadvantaged (29 percent among four-year colleges) ranks lower than that for racial/ethnic minorities (32 percent), athletes (32 percent), students with special nonacademic talents (37 percent), and academically talented students (57 percent).

THE AMERICAN PUBLIC

To gauge public views on this important topic, we conducted, on behalf of the Educational Testing Service, an extensive examination of public views about affirmative action, through a nationwide poll of more than 2,100 adults in October 1999, in partnership with Princeton Survey Research Associates. That telephone survey, the ETS/PSRA survey for short, included a series of questions to assess general attitudes about opportunity and success in life, as well as about a range of possible criteria that colleges and universities might use in their admissions decision.[22]

There is broad agreement that individual academic achievement, and the character traits of hard work and personal motivation it requires, should govern the distribution of opportunity in higher education. Yet, for most Americans the definition of academic merit also is contextual. While academic achievement is the primary measure of merit, high achievement in spite of disadvantages, especially low socioeconomic status, is viewed as especially meritorious and deserving. Nonetheless, in general the American opportunity narrative does

TABLE 3.6 FINANCIAL AID OFFERED TO ACCEPTED
APPLICANTS IN TWO-YEAR AND FOUR-YEAR INSTITUTIONS,
1979 AND 2000 (PERCENTAGE)

	Two-Year Institutions (Public and Private)		Four-Year Institutions (Public and Private)	
	1979	2000	1979	2000
NO-NEED AWARDS	51	61	51	61
MODIFIED PACKAGING	34	30	34	—
OFFERED TO:				
Athletes	51	32	51	32
Racial/ethnic minorities	26	32	26	32
Disadvantaged students	22	29	22	29
Students with special nonacademic talents	40	37	40	37
Academically talented students	61	57	61	57
Students from different geographic locations (within the United States)	12	20	12	20
International students	—	25	—	25
Students with disabilities	—	17	—	17
INSTITUTIONS RESPONDING TO QUESTIONNAIRE	1,463	1,644	1,463	1,644

Notes: 2000 summary data for this table were obtained from responses to questions 35 and 36 of the four-year questionnaire. Percentages are based on the total number of institutions responding to the questions.
Source: Breland et al., *Trends in College Admission 2000*.

not favor policies that give more weight to social or economic circumstances than academic credentials.

The public clearly views academic readiness as the primary consideration in admissions decisions but is willing to favor high-achieving, low socioeconomic status students over their similarly qualified peers. When presented with a series of alternative admissions strategies, the public dismissed lotteries, was ambiguous about race and ethnicity, and clearly supported strategies that mixed socioeconomic characteristics with academic merit—such as class rank within high schools or preferences for those students capable of rising above a background of deprivation.

Americans are still committed to economic and racial diversity in colleges. Although they do not favor admissions based on race all by itself, they do back admissions strategies that are mindful of their effects on racial and income diversity. Widespread public support for approaches that give priority to students whose grades give them high class rank in their respective high schools, irrespective of their test scores, is a case in point. High schools whose high-ranking students do not have commensurate test scores tend to be those with high concentrations of minorities or low-income students. The public also approves of outreach to low-income and minority students. Moreover, preferences for students from low-income families, which is where minority youth are concentrated, are popularly accepted.

Almost two-thirds of Americans favor preferences for equally qualified low-income students over higher-income students. About one-third favor preferences for low-income students even when they have slightly lower grades and test scores compared with students from high-income families.

Americans also strongly associate affirmative action with racial preferences and do not view racial preferences favorably. Among white Americans, 52 percent say affirmative action should be abolished,[23] and more than 80 percent oppose preference in hiring and promotions for racial minorities, even when the programs may help compensate for "past discrimination."[24]

At the same time, other research that has found that Americans endorse policies that promote upward mobility for high-achieving students from poor and working-class backgrounds.

Americans associate disadvantage with income more than with race. Low-income status is considered by 83 percent of those surveyed to be a disadvantage. A majority of respondents said being black or Hispanic is a disadvantage if the person also is from a low-income family. Notably, while few said being white is a disadvantage in itself, 71 percent said being white and from a low-income family is a disadvantage. Growing up in a family that does not speak English or growing up in a single-parent family were seen as major drawbacks in America as well. Being Hispanic or African American was regarded as a disadvantage by roughly half of those polled (see Table 3.7).

Americans recognize the link between higher education and success. In the author's own polling, respondents said educational institutions have the primary role among American institutions for promoting upward mobility. As Table 3.8 (page 124) illustrates, Americans vest immense importance in education. By a wide margin, respondents to the ETS/PSRA survey said public schools should play a primary role in helping young people get ahead in life. Colleges and universities, too, shoulder a big responsibility in the public mind

TABLE 3.7 WHAT HELPS AND HURTS IN LIFE?

	Considered an Advantage (percentage)	Considered a Disadvantage (percentage)
Not getting a college education	7	87
Going to a low-quality/ low-income high school	7	85
Growing up in a family that doesn't speak English	8	84
Growing up in a low-income family	10	83
Growing up in a single-parent family	7	80
Growing up in a low-income black family	7	78
Growing up in a low-income Hispanic family	6	77
Growing up in a low-income white family	12	71
Being Hispanic	19	51
Being African American	21	49
Being white	57	13
Growing up in a wealthy family	73	15

Source: ETS/PSRA Survey (1999).

for nurturing young people's success. The public ranks schools—especially public schools and colleges—far ahead of government, business and industry, churches, and the military as the institutions most responsible for equipping people with the tools needed to make the most of their opportunities.

ETS/PSRA survey respondents were nearly unanimous that—in principle—society should help less fortunate people get ahead in life, as Table 3.9 (page 124) illustrates. Among respondents, 91 percent agreed that people who start out with little and work their way up are the "real success stories." There was equally strong agreement that society should help people who are working hard to overcome disadvantages. The survey also shows how strongly the American public rejects the notion of not helping those in need. Seventy-two percent disagreed

TABLE 3.8 A PRIMARY ROLE FOR SCHOOLS IN HELPING YOUNG PEOPLE GET AHEAD?

	These institutions should play . . .		
	a primary role (percentage)	some role (percentage)	no role (percentage)
Public schools	72	26	2
Public colleges/universities	61	35	2
Private colleges/universities	47	45	5
Business and industry	39	53	5
Faith-based organizations	39	52	7
Government	38	46	15
Military	24	53	5

Source: ETS/PSRA Survey (1999).

TABLE 3.9 AMERICAN VALUES AND OPPORTUNITY

	Agree (percentage)	Disagree (percentage)
We should help people who are working hard to overcome disadvantages and succeed in life.	93	6
People who start out with little and work their way up are the real success stories.	91	7
Some people are born poor, and there's nothing we can do about that.	26	72
We shouldn't give special help at all, even to those who started out with more disadvantages than most.	16	81

Source: ETS/PSRA Survey (1999).

with the statement that there is nothing society can do about people who are born poor. An even larger majority—81 percent—disagreed with the premise that, no one, even if starting out "with more disadvantages than most," should receive special help.

Most Americans accept the notion that, at least in some cases, students from low-income families should be given extra consideration in college admissions. As Table 3.10 illustrates, 65 percent in the ETS/PSRA survey said qualified low-income students should sometimes or always have an advantage over equally qualified students who are not from low-income families. About one-third said that should happen only rarely or never.

If a rich and a poor student are equally qualified, whom should a college admit? Americans overwhelmingly favor the less privileged student over the wealthier student, as Table 3.11 (page 126) reports.

But, according to Table 3.12 (page 126), public opinion shifts significantly if the low-income student has slightly lower test scores than the student from a more affluent family. Only one-third of survey respondents would then admit that low-income student, compared to two-thirds who would choose the low-income student if scores were equal.

TABLE 3.10

How often, if ever, do you think qualified students from low-income families should have an advantage over equally qualified students who are not from low-income families in getting into a college or university?

	Percentage
Always	15
In some cases	50
Only rarely	15
Never	16
Depends	1

Source: ETS/PSRA Survey (1999).

TABLE 3.11

Two students have an "A" average in high school and get the same score on college admissions tests. If there is only one seat available, which student would you admit to college?

	Percentage
Student from low-income family	63
Student from high-income family	3
Both/neither	12
Don't know	20

Source: ETS/PSRA Survey (1999).

TABLE 3.12

If there is only one seat available, which student would you admit to college, the high-income student or the low-income student?

	Percentage
Both students get the same admissions test score	
Low-income student	63
High-income student	3
The low-income student gets a slightly lower score	
Low-income student	33
High-income student	54
The low-income student also is black, and the high-income student is white	
Low-income student	36
High-income student	39
The low-income student also is Hispanic, and the high-income student is not	
Low-income student	33
High-income student	45

Source: ETS/PSRA Survey (1999).

Among ETS/PSRA survey respondents with family incomes of less than $30,000, 73 percent would give low-income students an admissions advantage, at least in some cases, over equally qualified students who are not from low-income families. By contrast, 60 percent of those with family incomes of $50,000 or more would give low-income students a special break.

Among Democrats in the ETS/PSRA survey, 72 percent believe low-income students should, at least in some cases, have an edge in college admissions, compared to 64 percent of independents and 60 percent of Republicans. Thus, while support varies, there is strong support even among Republicans and the wealthy for providing low-income students with a boost.

Although public opinion toward financing strategies to promote opportunity varies considerably, a large majority of Americans support increased funding for programs to help students from low-income families get a college education. As Table 3.13 (page 128) indicates, 81 percent favor additional state funding to make sure all students can take classes to prepare for college admissions tests like the SAT or ACT. Nearly as many support augmented funding for scholarship and loan programs and for offering college credit or advanced placement courses in high schools.

DATA ON DEFINING OBSTACLES BY SOCIOECONOMIC STATUS AND RACE

If college admissions officers and the American public agree that "merit" should be defined as achievement in light of obstacles overcome, what do the social science data say about the role of obstacles like low socioeconomic status and racial minority background?

SOCIOECONOMIC STATUS

Youth in higher-income families with college-educated parents are doubly privileged. They find college, especially the more expensive highly selective colleges, more affordable. More important, their childhood and adolescent development are nested in neighborhoods, high-quality schools, and home environments that provide the necessary social support, encouragement, and information to smooth their progress toward college.

TABLE 3.13 HELPING LOW-INCOME STUDENTS GET
A COLLEGE EDUCATION

	Favor (percentage)	Oppose (percentage)
Increased funding for SAT and ACT exam prep classes	81	17
Increased funding for scholarships and loans	79	18
Increased funding for A.P. classes in all high schools	78	17
Increased funding for college tutoring and counseling	73	24
An increase in state or local taxes	42	55
An increase in tuition at state universities	29	66

Source: ETS/PSRA Survey (1999).

As the strength of the relationship between education and income grows, families with the highest incomes are increasingly likely to be those in which parents have the highest level of educational attainment. Conversely, low-income families with increasing frequency are the ones headed by parents with low education levels. Our nation is increasingly clustered into families with both high parental education and elevated incomes and those with neither. As a result, two roads to college are converging into a single, narrower pathway. In the early post–World War II era, blue-collar men with union jobs had sufficient income to live in neighborhoods with good schools and other forms of supportive social capital for their children, from libraries to public safety to peer support among students from upwardly mobile families. Many of these students went on to college even though their parents had high school educations or less. At the same time, there were families with relatively high levels of parental education but less income. The children of schoolteachers, for instance, went on to college primarily because of high parental expectations for their education. With the economic reward to education growing and becoming more concentrated, access to college and choices among colleges by price and selectivity will become more polarized by income class, and low-income African American and Hispanic families will suffer the greatest deprivation.

Most researchers agree that the relationship between parental education and income creates a virtuous intergenerational circle of success. Simply put, parental education brings strong returns to household income, which in turn tends to raise time and resource investments in children and educational expectations. This contributes to higher rates of high school completion and readiness for college. Those who are most ready are more likely to enroll and to graduate. Those who graduate tend to get good jobs with long-term earnings potential. Their children are raised in households with both strong earnings and high levels of parental education, continuing the virtuous circle into the next generation.

Diminished educational expectations are especially prevalent in families of low socioeconomic status. Among eighth-grade students surveyed in 1988, 42 percent of those from families in the lowest socioeconomic status quartile aspired to bachelor's degrees, compared to 64 percent of students from the middle two quartiles and 89 percent of top-quartile students.[25] These expectations drive students' motivation to take the necessary steps to attend a top-tier, highly selective college as well as their performance on college entrance exams. Students from families who expect their children to attend a four-year college—about one-third of the total—were more inclined to take the SAT or ACT and were more likely to score higher when they did so than students whose families had lower expectations.[26]

The obstacles students in low-income families face are so significant that just 7 percent from the bottom socioeconomic status quartile scored in the top 25 percent of NELS exam takers. By contrast, 50 percent of those from families in the highest socioeconomic status quartile scored in the top fourth of test takers on the exam. At the opposite extreme, 39 percent of students from low socioeconomic status families, compared with 8 percent from high socioeconomic status families, were in the bottom NELS quartile.[27]

The pool of students with high scores on college entrance exams is highly skewed by socioeconomic status. Nearly two out of three students who post higher than an SAT-equivalent score of 1300—that is, in the highest 8 percent—are from the top socioeconomic status quartile (see Table 3.14, page 130). Of those who score between 1200

TABLE 3.14 HIGH-SCORING STUDENTS ARE FROM THE
HIGHEST SES QUARTILE (PERCENTAGE)

	All	Non–Test Taker	<1000	1000–1100	1100–1200	1200–1300	>1300
First Quartile	25	37	21	8	6	4	3
Second Quartile	26	30	25	24	17	14	10
Third Quartile	26	22	30	32	29	23	22
Fourth Quartile	23	10	24	36	47	58	66

Source: Authors' analysis of NELS:88.

and 1300, 58 percent are from the top socioeconomic status quartile. By contrast, just 3 percent of those who score above 1300 and 4 percent of those who score between 1200 and 1300 come from the lowest socioeconomic status quartile.

These effects are compounded to the extent that residential patterns tend to segregate students by socioeconomic status among high schools. Students with higher socioeconomic status tend to go to high schools that are more successful in providing access to college, especially highly selective colleges. There is further segregation of students within high schools, with low socioeconomic status students less likely to take the more rigorous college preparatory curriculum. The separation of high and low socioeconomic status students, both among and within high schools, also reduces the positive "peer effects" that come from mixing youth with different social characteristics.[28]

American high schools vary widely in terms of qualifications of teachers, students' feelings of personal safety, amount of homework, and access to technology, as well as family, peer, and community support and expectations. But there are no accessible measures that differentiate high schools by their relative level of advantages. This chapter uses the share of students who receive subsidized lunches as a proxy for the peer influences of the high school. Do students from the same socioeconomic status quartile perform the same or not in different kinds of high schools?[29]

Richard Kahlenberg cites a variety of studies that show that younger children from low socioeconomic status families perform better if they attend high-income high schools.[30] In order to try to isolate the independent effects of class origin and the quality of the high school, we tracked how students from different kinds of families (socioeconomic status quartiles) performed at different types of high schools based on three levels of frequency of subsidized lunches (low-income high schools: greater than 30 percent; medium-income: 10 to 30 percent; and high-quality: 0 to 10 percent).

The resulting data support Kahlenberg's view, finding an inverse relationship between the percentage of students receiving subsidized lunches in high schools and the proportions who take college entrance exams. In high schools where no more than 10 percent receive subsidized lunches (high-income high schools), 64 percent take a college entrance exam, compared to only 37 percent in high schools where greater than 30 percent of the students receive subsidized lunches (low-income high schools). The same pattern is evident in the share of students who achieved above-average board scores. At high-income high schools, 40 percent of test takers had an SAT-equivalent score of 1000 or better versus 19 percent in low-income high schools.

Low socioeconomic status students do better in high-income high schools. Table 3.15 (page 132) reveals that only 24 percent of students in the bottom socioeconomic status quartile scored in the top half of the NELS test if they attended low-income high schools. By contrast, 36 percent of students from families in the bottom socioeconomic status quartile who attended high-income high schools were in the top half of the NELS test score distribution.

High school attended affects the selectivity of four-year colleges that students choose. According to Table 3.16 (page 133), one-half of the college students from both the lowest socioeconomic status families and the lowest-income high schools went to the fourth-tier, less selective colleges (basically open admission); only 16 percent of these students went to a school in one of the top two tiers of selectivity. In contrast, low socioeconomic status college students from high-income high schools were more likely to attend top-tier, highly selective colleges: 30 percent went to a college in one of the top two tiers, whereas only 21 percent registered with fourth-tier schools.

TABLE 3.15 EFFECT OF HIGH SCHOOL SOCIOECONOMIC
STATUS ON SCHOLASTIC PERFORMANCE

Student SES Status	Type of High School	Share in Top Half of NELS Test
LOWEST SES QUARTILE:	High Income	36
	Medium Income	28
	Low Income	24
SECOND SES QUARTILE:	High Income	49
	Medium Income	28
	Low Income	24
THIRD SES QUARTILE:	High Income	64
	Medium Income	58
	Low Income	53
HIGHEST SES QUARTILE:	High Income	77
	Medium Income	68
	Low Income	70

Note: High income = less than 10 percent received subsidized lunch; Medium income = between 10 and 30 percent received subsidies; Low income = more than 30 percent subsidized.
Source: Authors' analysis of NELS:88.

RACE AND ETHNICITY

Our findings are analogous to many others showing that the inequality in educational opportunity among African Americans and Hispanics cannot be completely accounted for by socioeconomic status or by school variables. Race and ethnicity matter in the distribution of opportunity, independent of other characteristics. Socioeconomic status does not explain why 75 percent of those who live in neighborhoods with the highest concentrations of poverty are racial or ethnic minorities.[31] A close look at the data finds that 12 percent of Asians, 16 percent of whites, 25 percent of African Americans, and 29 percent of Hispanics go to high schools with the lowest share of students going on to four-year colleges. Similarly, 44 percent of Asians, 41 percent of whites, 16 percent of African Americans, and 14 percent of Hispanics go to high schools with the lowest share of students (0–10 percent) who get subsidized school lunches.

TABLE 3.16 SOCIOECONOMIC STATUS, HIGH SCHOOL, AND POST–HIGH SCHOOL EDUCATION (PERCENTAGE)

Student SES Status	High School Attended	No Post-secondary Education	Two-Year College	Four-Year College	College Selectivity			
					Highest	Second	Third	Lowest
LOWEST SES QUARTILE:	High Income	63	23	14	2	2	7	3
	Medium Income	67	21	12	1	1	5	4
	Low Income	65	21	13	0	2	5	7
SECOND SES QUARTILE:	High Income	44	32	25	1	5	12	6
	Medium Income	47	34	20	2	3	8	7
	Low Income	50	25	24	1	6	10	8
THIRD SES QUARTILE:	High Income	29	28	43	5	7	22	9
	Medium Income	32	25	42	5	8	20	9
	Low Income	31	29	39	2	8	19	11
HIGHEST SES QUARTILE:	High Income	10	26	64	22	16	16	10
	Medium Income	16	23	61	12	9	24	16
	Low Income	17	19	63	13	9	26	16

Note: High income = less than 10 percent received subsidized lunch; Medium income = between 10 and 30 percent received subsidies; Low income = more than 30 percent subsidized.
Source: Authors' analysis of NELS:88

Blacks and Hispanics make up a higher proportion of those who attend high schools with the lowest rates of college attendance, the most widespread incidence of subsidized school lunches, and the least "social capital" (see Figure 3.1). While non-Hispanic whites constitute 65 percent of the students at schools where the fewest students go directly to four-year colleges, they account for 77 percent of the population of schools where at least a majority attends such colleges. The difference is even greater when schools are differentiated by percentage of students who receive subsidized lunches. Whites are 84 percent of the student body at schools with the fewest subsidized students and 49 percent of schools where more students receive subsidies. By way of contrast, blacks are 6 percent of the student body at schools with the fewest subsidized students and 24 percent at schools where more students receive subsidized lunches.

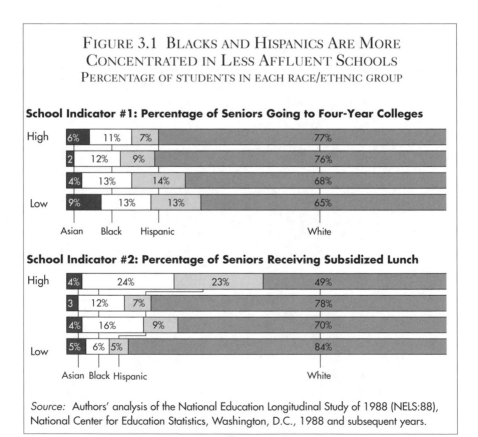

FIGURE 3.1 BLACKS AND HISPANICS ARE MORE
CONCENTRATED IN LESS AFFLUENT SCHOOLS
PERCENTAGE OF STUDENTS IN EACH RACE/ETHNIC GROUP

School Indicator #1: Percentage of Seniors Going to Four-Year Colleges

High
6% | 11% | 7% | 77%
2 | 12% | 9% | 76%
4% | 13% | 14% | 68%
Low
9% | 13% | 13% | 65%

Asian   Black   Hispanic   White

School Indicator #2: Percentage of Seniors Receiving Subsidized Lunch

High
4% | 24% | 23% | 49%
3 | 12% | 7% | 78%
4% | 16% | 9% | 70%
Low
5% | 6% | 5% | 84%

Asian Black Hispanic   White

Source: Authors' analysis of the National Education Longitudinal Study of 1988 (NELS:88), National Center for Education Statistics, Washington, D.C., 1988 and subsequent years.

The corresponding figures for Hispanics are 5 and 23 percent, respectively. The broad dispersion of low-income whites and the isolation of low-income minorities is compelling evidence of the persistence of racial stigma.

The view that race should not matter reflects a narrow moral stance. It relies solely on a procedural standard of equal treatment rather than a broader standard that considers actual roadblocks impeding the opportunity to learn in minority communities or the racial distribution of degrees from prestigious colleges.[32] It is what Michael Walzer calls "thin" morality, or the slavish, ahistorical adherence to an ideal. The contrasting position is the ability to compromise the ideal in order to see it fulfilled.[33] As Glenn C. Loury points out, correcting procedural discrimination does not correct for the effects of its violations.[34] What else but racial stigma explains the fact that 2 percent of black women between the ages of twenty-five and thirty-four years old are married to white men, compared with 39 percent of Hispanic women and 70 percent of Asian women?[35]

ECONOMIC AFFIRMATIVE ACTION

Given broad societal agreement among the public and college admissions officers that merit should be defined partly in terms of difficulties overcome, what sort of consideration of obstacles—racial and socioeconomic—is in fact given? Our own analysis finds that race and ethnicity is a significant consideration for colleges, boosting admissions from 4 percent under a system strictly of grades and test scores for African Americans and Latinos to 12 percent enrolled. By contrast, being economically disadvantaged, on net, reduces rather than improves chances of enrolling at one of the 146 most selective colleges. Admission based on tests and grades alone increases socioeconomic diversity marginally, from the current 9 to 12 percent from the bottom half of the income distribution.

The critical question becomes, If colleges provided an admissions break to students from lower socioeconomic backgrounds, would these students be able to handle the work at selective colleges?

The conventional view that academic preparation is a monolithic barrier to access and choice among low socioeconomic status students is greatly overstated and an unnecessary barrier to policies that can have immediate effects. There are large numbers of students from families with low income and low levels of parental education who are academically prepared for bachelor's degree attainment, even in the most selective colleges. Their numbers are far larger than those who currently attend. According to NCES, low-income students who graduate from high school at least minimally qualified for college enroll in four-year institutions at half the rate of their high-income peers.[36]

Even among students who perform identically on the NELS test, those in a higher socioeconomic status category are more likely to take the SAT or ACT and are more likely to go to four-year colleges. Because scores on the NELS test correlate very closely with SAT-equivalent scores, this demonstrated that a number of students—as many as 300,000—with the apparent potential to achieve relatively high SAT-equivalent scores do not attend a four-year college. Among those in the top NELS test quartile but the lowest socioeconomic status quartile, fully 43 percent took neither the SAT nor the ACT, whereas only 13 percent of the high NELS scorers in the top socioeconomic status quartile did not take either test. Of those in both the top NELS test quartile and the top socioeconomic status quartile, 80 percent enrolled in a four-year college within two years after high school. By contrast, only 44 percent of those from the lowest socioeconomic status quartile who had high NELS test scores went directly to institutions granting bachelor's degrees. In fact, fully 31 percent did not attend any postsecondary institution.[37] They are the low-hanging fruit in any policy strategy to increase socioeconomic diversity in four-year colleges, including selective colleges.

The effect of socioeconomic status on postsecondary attendance is evident in the other quartiles of NELS test scores as well. In the second-highest test score quartile, 62 percent from the highest socioeconomic status quartile go directly to four-year colleges, while only 21 percent of those from the lowest socioeconomic status quartile make that transition. In fact, more than one-half of the latter group do not attend any postsecondary institution; the comparable figure for those in the top socioeconomic status quartile is 11 percent.

As Table 3.17 shows, not all of those who score high on tests enroll in the best colleges. Of those who had an SAT-equivalent score greater than 1300 and attended a four-year college, only 41 percent went to the 146 top-tier colleges. Twenty-two percent enrolled in second-tier colleges, 25 percent attended third-tier colleges, and 12 percent enrolled in fourth-tier institutions.

Even the elite colleges admit candidates with a wide range of SAT or ACT scores. Roughly 20 percent of test takers have an SAT-equivalent score above 1200. There are almost twice as many of these students as there are seats in the 146 top-tier colleges. In fact, looking at the flip side, only 57 percent of the students enrolling in these choice institutions had SAT-equivalent scores above 1200; more than 14 percent scored less than 1100. Because of the joint preferences of students themselves and the colleges they attend, top-tier colleges do not simply consist of high-scoring students.[38]

Even though top-tier colleges have high graduation rates, there appears to be some minimal level of readiness needed. While these institutions do not admit many students with SAT-equivalent scores below 1000, those who do enroll are not nearly as successful as students with higher scores. Only 61 percent of students admitted to these institutions with a combined SAT-equivalent score of between 900 and 1000 graduate, and this figure drops to 30 percent when the scores are below 900. While a 61 percent graduation rate is in line with the overall college graduation rate of 65 percent, it is considerably lower than the 86 percent graduation rate of those students in elite colleges with SAT-equivalent scores between 1000 and 1200 (or the 95 percent graduation rate for those with SAT-equivalent scores greater than 1200). Thus, students with scores below 1000 stand out as a less successful group in this setting.

TABLE 3.17 ALL COLLEGES ADMIT STUDENTS WITH A WIDE RANGE OF SAT-EQUIVALENT SCORES (PERCENTAGE)

	Non–Test Taker	<1000	1000–1100	1100–1200	1200–1300	>1300	Total
Tier 1	9	7	7	20	31	26	100
Tier 2	15	15	19	25	15	11	100
Tier 3	12	43	19	21	9	6	100
Tier 4	22	37	15	15	5	6	100
2-Year Colleges	55	28	8	7	1	0	100

Source: Authors' analysis of NELS:88.

To put these scores in perspective, about half of the high school graduating class takes the SAT or the ACT. These students tend to come from the upper half of academic performers in the class. Roughly half of those score above 1000 on the SAT or achieve an equivalent score on the ACT. The total number of students who score above 1000, the top quarter of the nation's high school graduating class, is about 812,000, or four and a half times as many as there are places in at the elite colleges.

Current practice demonstrates that the qualified pool for selecting students at the top 146 colleges includes all students who score 1000 or better on the SAT or its equivalent on the ACT. The freshman classes at the selective Tier I colleges include only about 7 percent who come in below a 1000 SAT equivalent. But this gives a qualified pool that is almost five times the number of seats in selective colleges. Because there are many more students academically qualified to go to selective institutions, the standards of choice among them are necessarily complex and controversial. The real question in admissions at selective colleges is, "Who is deserving?"

The reality that many high school students from low socioeconomic status families are qualified for college but do not attend or go to colleges that are less selective than their achievements justify is not widely recognized. The conventional view is that students from low-income families, especially those with low levels of parental education, do not enroll in college, fail to persevere to graduation, or shy away from enrolling in selective colleges because they are not academically suited for the rigors.

Although a family history of deprivation reduces the likelihood that students will be academically prepared to go to college, a substantial share do enroll and graduate nonetheless. Moreover, those high-achieving secondary school students from low socioeconomic status families who have attended four-year and highly selective colleges have performed well in terms of grades and graduation rates when compared to similarly qualified students from high socioeconomic status families.

SIMULATION OF ALTERNATIVE ADMISSIONS STRATEGIES

This section examines five alternative practices for creating pools of students qualified for admission to four-year and selective colleges: those with the highest grades and test scores; a lottery with minimum academic qualifications; those with the highest class rank; a class rank plan with minimum academic qualifications; and affirmative action for low-income students. It assesses the impact of each alternative on the racial, ethnic, socioeconomic status, and academic makeup of pools of students qualified for admission.

In all of these approaches, a minimum standard of readiness is set that assumes a minimum SAT-equivalent score of 900 (the NCAA minimum) when simulating the effects of lotteries. In analyzing class rank (top 10 or 20 percent), options are simulated without a minimum SAT-equivalent test score and with a minimum SAT-equivalent score of 1000. Affirmative action for low-income students also uses a 1000 SAT-equivalent minimum. The simulated national pools assume that all those who exceed 1300 also will be included. Hence, the focus is on the 1000–1300 pool generated by the parameters of the different admission models. One thousand was the logical choice as the minimum score in most of the simulations because those who range above 1000 tend to come from the top 25 percent of their graduating class from high school, because 1000 tends to be around the median of the ACT and SAT score distribution, and because students at top-tier colleges with an SAT-equivalent score below 1000 have substantially lower graduation rates.

Any admissions plan that let in a large group of these sub-1000 students would be criticized as "lowering standards" too much. At the same time, among those scoring between 1000 and 1100, 86 percent graduated, a rate not substantially below the 96 percent graduating among those who score above 1300 (see Table 3.2, page 108).

It is important to note that these simulations are more a thought experiment than a true representation of what actually takes place in the admissions office at selective colleges. They do not reflect the complexity of the real college admissions process. They do not include a wide variety of criteria from the need to fill up classes in Greek to the demand for oboe or field hockey players. In addition, while this chapter considers each alternative approach separately, actual admissions policies use multiple standards applied differentially to diverse groups of applicants at varying stages of the admissions and financial aid processes.

ALTERNATIVE APPROACHES TO ADMISSIONS

This section begins by looking at the baseline enrollments of the entering class at the 146 most selective colleges. Then the effects of five alternative approaches to admissions are simulated.

ALTERNATIVE 1—Highest grades, test scores, teacher recommendations, and demonstrated leadership. This is a model in which admissions decisions are based exclusively on the most easily quantifiable academic measures, including grades, college entrance exam scores, teacher recommendation, and participation and leadership in extracurricular activities;

ALTERNATIVE 2—Lottery with minimal academic qualifications. All students with an SAT-equivalent score greater than 900 are considered eligible for the admissions pool at the 146 most selective colleges;

ALTERNATIVE 3—Class rank. All students who finish in the top 10 or 20 percent of their high school class;

ALTERNATIVE 4—Class rank with minimum academic qualifications. All students in the top 10 or 20 percent of their class who also scored a minimum of 1000 on their SAT or the equivalent on the ACT;

ALTERNATIVE 5—Academically qualified but low socioeconomic status students. All students with high academic achievement, outstanding teacher recommendations, and evidence of participation and leadership in extracurricular activities who come from less privileged families and poorer high schools.

Each of these five alternatives to college admissions will be evaluated according to four criteria:

CRITERION 1—Public Approval. Using data from their own opinion survey, we assess the extent to which each approach meets with public approval;

CRITERION 2—Racial and Ethnic Diversity. The shares and numbers of minorities, especially African Americans and Hispanics, within the qualifying pool;

CRITERION 3—Socioeconomic Diversity. The shares of qualifying students from families in the top socioeconomic status quartile and the bottom two socioeconomic status quartiles;

CRITERION 4—College Performance. The likelihood of graduating from a selective college.

The Current Enrollment Baseline

CRITERION 1—Public Approval. By and large, Americans support college admissions strategies based on academic merit and special talents from the French horn to football. They also support recognition of background traits that demonstrate striving, but most are uncomfortable with or opposed to admission based solely on race or ethnicity.

CRITERION 2—Racial and Ethnic Diversity. Enrollments at the 146 colleges were composed of roughly 6 percent Hispanics, 6 percent African Americans, 12 percent Asian Americans, and the remainder non-Hispanic whites in the base year of 1995 as well as in a parallel analysis by Michael T. Nettles, Catherine M. Millett, and Marne K. Einarson using 1997 data.[39]

CRITERION 3—Socioeconomic Diversity. Most students (74 percent) in the most selective colleges come from families in the highest socioeconomic status quartile. Roughly 10 percent come from the bottom two socioeconomic status quartiles, and only 3 percent come from the bottom income quartile. There is thus more demographic than economic diversity at selective colleges.

CRITERION 4—College Performance. Eighty-six percent of students finished their four-year degree at selective colleges.

Alternative 1: Highest Grades, Test Scores, Teacher Recommendations, and Leadership

At one extreme, the "most" and "highly" selective colleges can create qualified pools that include only the most academically qualified students by relying on the measurable criteria of grades and entrance exam scores. Teacher recommendations and extracurricular activities also can be included. But the effect of teacher recommendations and extracurricular activities on inclusion in the qualified pool is unlikely to be large because there are many more candidates with solid teacher recommendations and extensive extracurricular activities than students with high grades and test scores.

CRITERION 1—Public Approval. There is widespread support for using grades and test scores in college admissions decisions. In our survey, 44 percent say grades and test scores should be very important in admissions, 49 percent say somewhat important, and only 6 percent say grades and test scores should not be considered important.

CRITERION 2—Racial and Ethnic Diversity. Using these more narrow criteria sharply limits the opportunity for minorities to qualify. In this case only 1.6 percent of the eligible pool are African American and 2.4 percent are Hispanic, a considerable drop from the current 6 percent share for each group.[40] This approach is the only one that would actually reduce the number of black and Hispanic students in the qualified pool (10,400) below the enrollment levels (15,100) in 1995 and 1997.

One interesting finding in this simulation is that the share of Asians in the eligible pool drops almost in half, from 12 percent to 7 percent, in the grades/scores approach compared with the base year as well as with the 1997 data from Nettles, Millett, and Einarson. It was noted earlier that not all high scorers go to the best schools. However, among high scorers Asians are much more likely to enroll in one of the top 146 colleges than others. They also come from the most affluent families and attend high schools with the lowest proportion of students with subsidized school lunches and the highest share of students who go on to four-year colleges.

CRITERION 3—Socioeconomic Diversity. Using grades and test scores as the criteria for creating the qualified selection pool increases socioeconomic status diversity. The share of students from the bottom two socioeconomic status quartiles would increase slightly from the base level of almost 10 percent to 12 percent. While the share of students from low socioeconomic status families would increase, seven out of eight matriculating selective schools would still come from the top half of the income distribution.

CRITERION 4—College Performance. More than 90 percent of students with high test scores and grades would graduate if admitted to one of the top-tier colleges or universities, a relatively small increase of 4 percent over current levels.

ALTERNATIVE 2: LOTTERY WITH MINIMAL ACADEMIC QUALIFICATIONS

One approach for raising both social and socioeconomic diversity in top colleges is to rely on a lottery of all qualified students (as measured by a minimum test score). In the extreme case, if there were no academic requirements, a lottery of all eighteen-year-olds would reflect the racial, ethnic, and socioeconomic status composition of American youth. Of course, the graduation rates of groups chosen without any regard to academic qualifications could be expected to be far lower than those actually in evidence at present, and this would surely be regarded as unsatisfactory by the colleges involved.

Some support lotteries among applicants qualified by a minimum set of scores and grades.[41] The underlying logic of this approach is that many more students are capable of keeping up at the top colleges than there are seats available, and all of these students should have a chance of getting this superior education. For instance, based on historical experience, anyone who achieves an SAT-equivalent score above 900 has at least a 69 percent chance of graduating from one of the 146 most selective colleges.

The lottery admission proposal for the 146 "most" and "highly" selective colleges was modeled by looking at all students with a minimum SAT-equivalent score of 900. The 900 cutoff is somewhat arbitrary but was chosen, in part, because it roughly matches the current standard set by the NCAA for student athletes.

CRITERION 1—Public Approval. The survey showed that fully 83 percent of the public disagree with the idea that colleges and universities should use a lottery to choose which students are admitted. This finding is not surprising given our cultural bias in favor of individuals over groups and a strong preference for merit-based opportunity.

CRITERION 2—Racial and Ethnic Diversity. Using the lottery approach with a minimum SAT-equivalent score of 900 would not increase the share of minorities in the qualified pool over current levels. The resulting eligibility pool would be 5 percent black and 4 percent Hispanic. These ratios are slightly below those of the entering class of 1995 and those in the analysis by Nettles, Millett, and Einarson in 1997. The low shares of minorities in the qualified pool reflect the fact that blacks and Hispanics are much less likely than whites to take the

SAT or ACT or to score above 900 when they do. While the share of African Americans and Hispanics in the pool is smaller than current enrollments, the absolute size of the pool is so large that the number of blacks and Hispanics in the qualified pool is six times the number in the current enrollment base.

CRITERION 3—Socioeconomic Diversity. Socioeconomic diversity would increase substantially using a lottery to create the qualified pool, with only 45 percent coming from the top socioeconomic status quartile and 27 percent from the bottom two socioeconomic status quartiles.

CRITERION 4—College Performance. The lottery approach with a minimum score of 900 relies on a low standard—only 30 percent of test takers score below 900 in any case. As a result, it would likely result in dramatically reduced graduation rates or lowered standards in otherwise selective colleges.

ALTERNATIVE 3: CLASS RANK

Several states have recently announced a strategy designed to increase opportunity and diversity in their public universities without using race as a criterion by guaranteeing admission to all in-state students who graduate from high school in some top percentage of their class. Actual percentages vary among states: Texas uses 10 percent, Florida makes it 20 percent, and California, 4 percent. These guarantees are made without regard to scores on national college entrance examinations. Such programs have found favor among those who are looking for ways to balance merit and greater equality of opportunity to learn by race, ethnicity, and income level.

These "class rank" approaches narrow the merit-based competition for seats at selective colleges to individual high schools, thereby recognizing and partially compensating for the negative effects on school performance of racial and economic isolation. In one sense, the strategy represents a pragmatic compromise between the values of individual merit and opening avenues to success for racial, ethnic, and low-income groups. In concept, they represent a rough ordering of moral priorities. They are merit-based but not indifferent to the effect of admissions procedures on racial, ethnic, and class outcomes.

CRITERION 1—Public Approval. The public supports admissions plans that reward students who rank high in their own high schools. More than 75 percent of Americans agree that low-income students who get the best grades in their high school should be given preferences in admission to college (although existing class rank plans do not require beneficiaries to be poor). More than one-half agree that low-income students with the best grades or test scores in their high schools should be admitted, despite the fact that students in other high schools might have higher grades and scores.

CRITERION 2—Racial and Ethnic Diversity. Class rank approaches that apply to the top 10 or 20 percent of students in individual high schools appear to yield qualified pools whose minority concentrations are either slightly smaller or slightly larger than the actual enrollment shares in 1995 and 1997. Using the top 10 percent criteria, the qualified pool is 5 percent black and approximately 7 percent Hispanic. Using the top 20 percent criteria, resulting figures are 7 percent black and 8 percent Hispanic.

Class rank approaches create pools that are larger than the quantity of seats available. As a result, the sheer numbers of blacks and Hispanics in the pool are more impressive than their percentages of the whole when compared with the 1995 and 1997 enrollment levels. Taking a 10 percent plan, the numbers of blacks and Hispanics in the eligible pool double from a total of about fifteen thousand in 1995 to thirty thousand. The 20 percent pool would bring in an eye-popping 68,000 blacks and Hispanics nationwide.

CRITERION 3—Socioeconomic Diversity. High class rank approaches add social diversity to the eligibility pool of top colleges. Instead of three-quarters coming from the top socioeconomic status quartile, only 40 percent of high-ranking students at each high school taken together come from these families. In addition, fully 30 percent come from families in the bottom two socioeconomic status quartiles—three times the current share.

CRITERION 4—College Performance. The problem, however, is that not all of these students are prepared for the academic rigors at top schools. Absent remediation, a substantial share of students from the qualified pool may go to a selective four-year college yet may not ultimately attain a bachelor's degree. Many students with high class rank, especially if the

top 20 percent are considered, do not take college entrance exams—
usually an indicator that they have poor access to information resources
about postsecondary opportunities, low levels of social support, or short-
comings in their college-prep curriculum. Among students in the top 10
percent of their class, 16 percent do not take either the SAT or ACT, and
another 9 percent have an SAT-equivalent score under 1000. Comparable
figures for those in the top 20 percent are even higher: 18 percent do
not take a college entrance exam, and 15 percent score below 1000.

Students with high class rank in secondary school and high SAT
scores currently are going to selective colleges in large numbers and
performing nicely. But, as the data above show, almost one-quarter
of the top 10 percent and one-third of the top 20 percent have College
Board scores that predict that they would have comparatively less success in terms of earning a degree if they attended an elite institution. It
is precisely these students that would be the purported beneficiaries of
a program that guaranteed admission on the basis of class rank since
they would not have been admitted to a selective college under the
traditional criteria. These "extra" enrollees might have a graduation
rate as low as 50 percent, much lower than the current graduation
rate at selective colleges. Evidently, admission to elite schools on this
basis would not necessarily serve well many of the students in question.

Preparation issues are especially prominent for African Americans
and Hispanics. Among these minority individuals in the top 10 percent of their high school class, roughly one-quarter either do not take
a test or score below the SAT-equivalent of 1000. Among African
Americans and Hispanics in the top 20 percent of their high school
class, approximately one-half either do not take an admissions test or
score below 1000. The comparable figures for Asians and whites are 14
and 21 percent, respectively.

ALTERNATIVE 4: CLASS RANK WITH MINIMUM ACADEMIC QUALIFICATIONS

One way to minimize the low graduation rate found in class
rank schemes while maintaining public support for merit-based
admission is to add a college readiness requirement to them. The
modified class rank model only includes students who have an SAT-
equivalent score above 1000. This approach is consistent with the
public's desire to reward achievement (high class rank) and better
ensures that the students who are admitted are prepared to succeed.

CRITERION 1—Public Approval. Public support for plans that reward students who achieve in their own high schools would probably increase if class rank plans also carried a minimum performance standard.

CRITERION 2—Racial and Ethnic Diversity. The top 10 percent class rank alternative with minimum academic qualifications results in an eligibility pool that is 3 percent black and 4 percent Hispanic, not impressive when compared with the current enrollment baseline of roughly 6 percent each. The top 20 percent class rank alternative provides a similarly diminished representation of minority students: 4 percent Hispanics and 4 percent African Americans.

CRITERION 3—Socioeconomic Diversity. The added readiness requirement also will have a negative impact on the social class diversity of the eligibility pool of top colleges and universities. Nearly half of students from the top 10 percent and the top 20 percent of their high school class who attain minimal test qualifications come from high socioeconomic status families, compared with 27 percent who come from the bottom two socioeconomic status quartiles.

CRITERION 4—College Performance. Nearly 90 percent of students with both high class rank and minimum academic qualifications should graduate.

ALTERNATIVE 5: OUTREACH TO ACADEMICALLY QUALIFIED STUDENTS WITH LOW SOCIOECONOMIC STATUS BACKGROUNDS

In general, this analysis confirms two obvious facts about the American educational pipeline. First, the odds against students from less affluent families and schools, either in applying or being selected for entrance into selective colleges are higher than for students from better-off families and schools. Second, there are numerous students with the proven ability to beat those odds. By itself, admissions policy will not change the percentages drastically. Leveling the playing field is a challenge for education, economic, and social policymakers. But admissions policies can promote social mobility and student diversity by emphasizing outreach to students who have beaten the odds by overcoming their socioeconomic origins and their educational preparation in unfavorable school environments.

Such students meet at least three criteria. They are high achievers, as measured by their SAT-equivalent scores between 1000 and 1300 and a high school grade point average above 3.0 in core courses. They also demonstrate personal excellence, as evidenced by enthusiastic recommendations from teachers or leadership in extracurricular or community activities. Finally, they come from underprivileged families or struggling high schools. Underprivileged families are defined as those in the bottom 40 percent of the socioeconomic status scale used by the NCES. High schools are classified as struggling according to two measures: either a low percentage (less than 25 percent) of seniors going on to four-year colleges or a high percentage (greater than 25 percent) of students receiving lunch subsidies. The outreach model also includes a combined group in which a student must either meet the socioeconomic status criterion or have attended a high school matching one or both of the characteristics described above. Racial or ethnic characteristics do not enter into any of these definitions.

CRITERION 1—Public Approval. The public approves of color-blind outreach to qualified students who come from underprivileged families. If a low-income student and high-income student are equally qualified, fully 63 percent say the low-income student should be given priority in admissions.

CRITERION 2—Racial and Ethnic Diversity. An admission pool that includes high achievers from families and high schools that meet at least one of the special outreach criteria will have 11,400 blacks and 19,200 Hispanics. These figures are considerably higher than the current enrollment baseline of 7,600 African Americans and 7,500 Hispanics. So, a high number of qualified minority students are identified, but colleges will have to face the challenge of deciding which candidates to accept. Since the pool generally is considerably larger under the outreach model, the proportion of African Americans falls to 4 percent, while Hispanics maintain the same 6 percent share as with present enrollments. A system that includes additional characteristics of socioeconomic disadvantage not measured here, such as net worth or single-parent household status, might boost racial diversity further.[42]

CRITERION 3—Socioeconomic Diversity. Using any approach that identifies high achievers from less affluent families and high schools results in much greater socioeconomic diversity than any of the other approaches. The percentage of students in the bottom two socioeconomic status quartiles rises from 10 percent to 38 percent.

CRITERION 4—College Performance. These students are as likely to succeed as any other students with comparable academic backgrounds. One can expect slightly less than 90 percent to graduate if they enroll in one of the 146 most selective colleges. The research shows that students from less fortunate families and embattled high schools performed much like students from more advantageous circumstances in the same SAT-equivalent range. In both groups, slightly less than half earned bachelor's degrees, and almost 10 percent went on to graduate degrees. In the combined group of high achievers facing at least one set of educational hurdles, only 6 percent had no postsecondary education versus 9 percent for all students who scored between 1000 and 1300. This demonstrates that once high-performing students from low socioeconomic status families get the chance, they are able to succeed. The problem is that they are less likely to attend top-tier colleges in any case.

It should be noted that this model assumes a fairly aggressive use of economic affirmative action. The economic preference envisioned is roughly one-half the magnitude of the preference currently provided to African American and Latino students. But the percentage of students affected would be greater because the eligible population of beneficiaries (economically disadvantaged) is larger than the population currently benefiting from racial affirmative action (blacks and Latinos). The model assumes universities would be willing almost to quadruple the share from the bottom economic half (from 10 percent to 38 percent). The racial dividend of economic affirmative action would be smaller if fewer students received the economic preference.

Is this assumption realistic? The share of students admitted with very high test scores (an SAT-equivalent of above 1300) would remain roughly the same: 30–35 percent under the model, compared with 26 percent currently. And lower-income students would still remain underrepresented (38 percent from the bottom half rather than 50 percent). At the same time, the losers under the policy would mostly be upper-middle-class students of all races, and the winners would be lower-middle-class whites and minorities. The switch would alienate politically powerful groups and help less powerful constituencies, a difficult task, even though recent polls suggest broad public appeal for giving a preference to lower-income groups.[43]

Still, there is some evidence from California, Texas, and Florida, where racial affirmative action has been banned at public universities, that the higher education community will take aggressive steps, including economic affirmative action, to ensure racial diversity in a race-neutral manner if using race is not an option. Moreover, the model presented here assumes race-neutral recruiting, so bold outreach efforts by race or poverty concentrations could improve racial diversity beyond expectations, even if race is banned from admissions decisions themselves. A definition of economic disadvantage more advantageous to minorities than the one employed in the proposed model might be adopted.[44] Likewise, new efforts to reduce the racial gap at the K–12 level might work over the long run. But ultimately there is no better way to guarantee a certain level of racial diversity than by employing race per se.

POLICY RECOMMENDATIONS

Based on the findings presented here, four sets of policy recommendations follow: class rank plans are fraught with difficulty; economic affirmative action should be widely adopted; race-based affirmative action should be maintained; and financial aid policies must be reoriented toward need.

CLASS RANK APPROACHES ARE FRAUGHT WITH DIFFICULTY

Class rank approaches are a proven political winner, but serious reservations about the plans remain. They reflect an effective ordering of public values because merit is primary and explicit while race, ethnicity, and socioeconomic status are secondary and implicit. Yet these approaches, as has been seen, suffer from the fact that they include many students who will find the work at selective colleges difficult, discouraging persistence and limiting their choices in the curriculum. Class rank approaches tied to assessments that trigger remediation would improve readiness, although they reduce diversity.

Another problem with the class rank approach is "creaming," even within schools where most students come from lower socioeconomic status or minority backgrounds. Virtually all high schools include students from a variety of socioeconomic strata. As shown in Table 3.18, even in the least affluent high schools 32 percent of students come from the top two economic quartiles. Moreover, those in the top 10 percent by grades are disproportionately wealthy. Even in the poorest schools, nearly 60 percent of such high achievers come from families in the top two socioeconomic status quartiles. As a result, approaches that focus on class rank, high school quality, or low-income neighborhoods will tend to favor those within the pool who are better off in economic terms.

ECONOMIC AFFIRMATIVE ACTION SHOULD BE EXPANDED

There is a need for much more vigorous use of economic affirmative action. College admissions officers and the public sensibly say

TABLE 3.18 SOCIAL COMPOSITION OF HIGH SCHOOLS AND HIGH-RANKING STUDENTS

| | SES Quartiles (percentage) | | | |
	First	Second	Third	Fourth
ALL STUDENTS IN SCHOOLS BY PERCENTAGE RECEIVING SUBSIDIZED LUNCHES				
Low (0–10%)	14	23	30	33
Medium (10–30%)	26	31	27	16
High (>30%)	41	27	21	11
TOP 10 PERCENT				
All	11	19	29	41
Low (0–10%)	7	20	24	49
Medium (10–30%)	9	18	37	36
High (>30%)	22	20	31	28

Source: Authors' analysis of NELS:88.

that any definition of merit should be tempered by a consideration of obstacles overcome, yet low-income students are hugely underrepresented at selective colleges. Many more of them could be admitted and could then succeed.

Much of the solution simply involves aggressive outreach. The current public dialogue tends to emphasize the decisions that highly selective colleges make when choosing among applicants. But most decisions on college are made long before the admissions officers get into the act. Almost half of high school students do not go to any postsecondary institution immediately after high school. Even among those who do go to college, students and their families choose colleges more than colleges choose students.

In the public view, academic merit is primary, but a record of accomplishment on the part of disadvantaged students is deemed appropriate for giving preferences among qualified students. There is broad support for giving special consideration for high-performing disabled students and students from low-income families, especially single-parent families.

Moreover, preferences for low-income students can help promote racial diversity compared with a system of admissions based on grades and test scores. When all reported incomes are adjusted for family size, 41 percent of Hispanics, 33 percent of African Americans, and 14 percent of non-Hispanic whites are living in families with resources below the "minimum but adequate" level, as specified by the U.S. Department of Labor. In addition, there appear to be many African Americans and Hispanics who are qualified but do not go on to four-year colleges. The analysis developed for this paper found a total of roughly twelve thousand African Americans and Hispanics who scored in the top quartile of the NELS test but did not attend a four-year college directly after high school. There were another fourteen thousand African Americans and eighteen thousand Hispanics who were in the upper half of the NELS test score distribution who did not attend a four-year college directly after high school. Like low socioeconomic status students, African Americans and Hispanic students have higher threshold requirements for attending four-year colleges, even with affirmative action policies in place.

Using a socioeconomic status preference expands the pool of qualified minority students substantially. If all the minimally qualified minority students in the bottom half of the income distribution were admitted, as many as eleven thousand African Americans and fifteen thousand Hispanics might be added to those already in the most selective colleges, roughly doubling the current numbers. In addition, with African Americans and Hispanics represented disproportionately among the qualified pool of low socioeconomic status students, public support for campus diversity goals as well as the legal basis for such objectives, is enhanced because of income-based admissions are broadly deemed an acceptable policy and because low-income, minority students are chosen on the basis of multiple criteria rather than race alone.

Maintain Racial Affirmative Action

While socioeconomic preferences help produce some racial diversity, a credible procedure that can reproduce the level of diversity that exists in society today without purposely singling out African Americans and Hispanics at some point in the selection process has yet to be found. Qualified minority candidates represent a fairly small share of the talented students newly identified using class rank and socioeconomic status pools. The choice between race or income preference and merit is a false one in a system where admissions are already based on multiple criteria.

Income- and race-based policies have overlapping effects, but they are not the same. While African Americans and Hispanics are overrepresented among the poor, whites still constitute the majority of families, particularly those in the second-lowest quartile. The qualified pool of low socioeconomic status students increases the number of African Americans and Hispanics compared to current enrollments but not their share overall. Hence, income-based policies are not an effective substitute for conscious racial and ethnic enrollment targets, unless low-income African Americans and Hispanics can be chosen disproportionately from the qualified pool of low socioeconomic status students (employing a modest degree of affirmative action while preserving the overall race-neutral character of the approach) or chosen as a supplement to the typically middle- and upper-income African Americans and Hispanics currently enrolled.

For instance, our own simulation of the pool of qualified students from the bottom half of the socioeconomic status distribution includes all those who have an SAT score of 1000 or better (or an equivalent ACT score) as well as high grades, teacher recommendations, and proven leadership. The pool takes in one and a half times the number of African Americans as were actually enrolled at the time and more than two and a half times as many Hispanics. Yet, African Americans and Hispanics make up only 4.0 percent and 5.8 percent of the entire pool of qualified low socioeconomic status students, compared with their current 6 percent share of seats at elite colleges. As a result, unless they are chosen disproportionately from the pool or chosen in addition to those from middle- and high-income families already enrolled, African Americans would lose ground relative to their current share of seats in the most selective colleges, and Hispanics would barely maintain their place.

The total number of students who score above 1000, the top quarter of the nation's high school graduating class, is about 812,000, of whom 35,000 are African American and 31,000 are Hispanic. Overall these 66,000 minority students who meet the SAT-equivalent minimal qualification are roughly four times the actual 1995 enrollment for such groups. Approximately 30 percent of these African Americans and 50 percent of the Hispanics are from the bottom half of the family income distribution or attend a less privileged high school. Hence, policies that focus exclusively on admissions for disadvantaged students exclude 24,000 qualified but relatively well-off African Americans and 13,600 Hispanics in similar circumstances.

Moreover, affirmative action defines the policy debate over admissions to selective colleges. All other proposals for expanding access and choice are measured by their implications for affirmative action. As a result, any discussion of selective college admission gets hopelessly entangled in a thicket of race, partisan politics, and idealism. Opposition to affirmative action has become a bottleneck for exploring the role of socioeconomic status, or other nonracial categories of disadvantage, in admissions.

While the support is widespread for income-based policies, including income-based affirmative action, it is superficial and unorganized. In part, this is because the natural proponents of such policies in the liberal/labor and civil rights communities fear that such policies will be used in a political shell game to supplant race-based affirmative action. Hence, the lost momentum on affirmative action reduces the scope for instituting policies to promote opportunity for students from low-income families. Politically speaking, the best way to pursue economic affirmative action is as a supplement to, rather than a replacement for, racial affirmative action.

FINANCIAL AID POLICIES

Creating diverse pools of qualified students is a necessary but insufficient condition for increasing access to college for low-income majority and minority students. The costs of four-year colleges, especially selective colleges, still present a barrier.

Removing other kinds of obstacles to enrollment in four-year and selective colleges will only make matters worse for qualified low-income students if financial barriers remain. Compared with similarly qualified students from more affluent families, low-income students have higher financial threshold requirements for enrolling in four-year colleges, especially the more expensive selective colleges. They face greater loan burdens and are more debt averse. Financial barriers are even growing, as evidenced by the way the value of Pell Grants as a percentage of the costs of college attendance has fallen precipitously since the 1970s. College costs as a percentage of family income have remained stable among students in the top 40 percent of the family income distribution but have increased substantially for lower-middle- and low-income families. Unmet financial need—the total price tag minus all student aid—was roughly equivalent across income classes in the 1974–75 school year and is still the same for high-income families but has since doubled for low-income families.

Huge numbers of low-income and minority students already are prepared for college but are either unable to afford it altogether, unable to attend the more selective and expensive colleges, or unable to make ends meet until graduation. These students do not need better preparation. Their problem can be handled in the short term by shrinking unmet financial need to the levels achieved in the early 1970s.

Barriers arise in the process of determining financial aid as well as the overall size and composition of the aid package. The practice of making financial aid decisions after admissions are completed discourages low-income students from applying to college, especially the more expensive selective colleges. In addition, the excessive loan burdens in student aid packages foisted on low-income students discourage applications as well. For those who manage to enroll anyway and stay on course until graduation, from four-year colleges, the problem is most acute.

Front-loading aid decisions and enhancing the grant portions of aid packages is an obvious solution. Moving up admissions and aid decisions for low-income students would require outreach as soon as early high school years, a critical juncture in academic preparation and the formation of college expectations. Front-loading federal Pell Grants as well as state and college aid would defer the need to take out loans and would move toward an equalization of risks and loan burdens between low-income and high-income students.

In order to ensure that such policies did not create disproportionate incentives to attend two-year and proprietary programs, grant aid would only apply to the first half of the required tenure for degree attainment. Hence, the first year of a two-year program and the first two years of a four-year program would be paid for with direct assistance. Front-loading aid for the first year of two-year programs and the first two years of four-year programs would encourage the development of more coherent and low-cost pathways from two-year colleges, where low-income and minority students are concentrated, to four-year schools.

Meeting the financial need of low-income students is in keeping with popular conceptions of merit and has strong public support. Need-based aid policies, coupled with admissions criteria that reflect a dynamic view of merit, are fully consistent with the American principle of opportunity for all who strive to excel.

APPENDIX

PELL GRANT RECIPIENTS IN SELECTIVE COLLEGES AND UNIVERSITIES[1]

Donald E. Heller

Little is known about the income distribution of students in specific colleges and universities in the United States. Institutions are required by law to report enrollment data by race and ethnicity to the U.S. Department of Education, but there is no such requirement regarding the enrollment of students from different income groups. While surveys conducted for the department provide a good portrait of the income stratification of students across different types of institutions nationally, these data cannot be used to ascertain the distribution for any single institution.

The department does provide data, however, on the number of Pell Grant recipients at every institution in the country. Receipt of a Pell Grant is a good proxy for estimating the family income of students. For example, the most recent data available from the National Postsecondary Student Aid Study, a representative survey of students conducted for the department in the 1999–2000 academic year, indicates that 90 percent of all dependent Pell Grant recipients in four-year institutions came from families with incomes below $41,000, and 75 percent of all Pell Grant recipients had family incomes below $32,000. While these exact proportions cannot be compared to all families nationally, data from the 2000 Census can be used to approximate the distribution of all families with children under eighteen years. In 1999, approximately 41 percent of all families with children had incomes below $40,000, and 29 percent had incomes below $30,000. Thus, it is clear that the average household income of Pell Grant recipients is much lower than that of families with children in the nation as a whole.

The tables that follow provide the undergraduate enrollment, number of Pell Grant recipients, and proportion of undergraduates receiving Pell Grants for the 2001–2002 academic year. They supply this information for *Barron's* "most competitive" (Table A.1, pp. 160–61) and "highly competitive" (Table A.2, pp. 162–66) institutions, along with a select number of institutions added to each list.[2]

The proportion of Pell Grant recipients ranged from zero (three institutions did not enroll any) to a high of roughly 35 percent of undergraduates at Rutgers University and the University of California, Los Angeles. The average frequency of Pell Grant beneficiaries among the undergraduate population in these institutions was 14 percent. The "most competitive" institutions on average had 10 percent of their undergraduates awarded Pell Grants, while 16 percent of students in the "highly competitive" institutions were recipients.

Public institutions, with an average Pell Grant enrollment of 19 percent of undergraduates, had a higher proportion than did their private counterparts, at 13 percent. Among public institutions, the University of California, Los Angeles, had the highest Pell Grant enrollment (35.1 percent of undergraduates), while the University of Virginia and the College of William and Mary had less than 9 percent of their undergraduates as beneficiaries.

Among private institutions, besides the three that enrolled no Pell Grant recipients (Grove City College, Jewish Theological Seminary, and the Webb Institute), Washington and Lee University and the University of Richmond each had 5 percent or less of their students receiving Pell Grants. At the other end of the scale, Brigham Young University and Lyon College each had more than 30 percent of their undergraduates in this category.

These figures can best be understood by placing them in the context of Pell Grant awards in four-year institutions nationally. In 1999–2000, the most recent academic year for which national data are available, 20 percent of dependent undergraduate students in public and private four-year institutions received Pell Grants. If community colleges are included, the figure dips to 18 percent.[3]

These data do not provide a perfect picture of the patterns of family income for students in selective institutions in the United States. For example, the upper limit of Pell Grant eligibility approaches the median family income across the nation ($50,000 in 1999). But, as noted earlier, 75 percent of dependent Pell recipients come from families with incomes below $32,000.[4]

In addition, Pell Grant eligibility is a better indicator of income status than the often-used marker of eligibility for financial aid. The latter descriptor can include, depending on how the phrase is used by institutions, students who are candidates for non-means-tested forms of aid, such as unsubsidized loans, privately originated loans, and merit scholarships.

For instance, while the median family income of all dependent Pell Grant recipients in four-year institutions nationally in 1999–2000 was $23,340, the median household income of students who received *any* form of financial aid was $53,413, or more than double. Seventy percent of all students in these institutions were offered some form of aid.

Tables begin on page 160.

TABLE A.1 MOST COMPETITIVE INSTITUTIONS

INSTITUTION	UNDER-GRADUATE ENROLLMENT	PELL GRANT RECIPIENTS (NUMBER)	PELL GRANT RECIPIENTS (PERCENTAGE)	NOTES
Amherst College, MA	1,640	259	15.8	
Barnard College/Columbia University, NY	2,261	417	18.4	
Bates College, ME	1,767	153	8.7	
Boston College, MA	9,797	1,038	10.6	
Bowdoin College, ME	1,635	166	10.2	
Brown University, RI	5,999	583	9.7	
California Institute of Technology, CA	942	144	15.3	
Carnegie Mellon University, PA	5,310	603	11.4	
Claremont McKenna College, CA	1,044	151	14.5	
Colby College, ME	1,809	117	6.5	
Colgate University, NY	2,814	294	10.4	
College of the Holy Cross, MA	2,811	241	8.6	
College of William and Mary, VA	5,604	450	8.0	
Columbia University, NY	6,867	1,023	14.9	
Cooper Union, NY	878	150	17.1	
Cornell University, NY	13,784	2,253	16.3	
Dartmouth College, NH	4,118	447	10.9	
Davidson College, NC	1,673	107	6.4	
Duke University, NC	6,203	629	10.1	
Georgetown University, DC	6,422	691	10.8	
Georgia Institute of Technology, GA	11,043	1,375	12.5	
Grove City College, PA	2,316	0	0.0	
Harvard University, MA	9,637	655	6.8	
Harvey Mudd College, CA	706	81	11.5	
Haverford College, PA	1,138	152	13.4	
Johns Hopkins University, MD	5,370	517	9.6	
Massachusetts Institute of Technology, MA	4,213	523	12.4	
Middlebury College, VT	2,328	189	8.1	

TABLE A.1 MOST COMPETITIVE INSTITUTIONS, CONT.

INSTITUTION	UNDER-GRADUATE ENROLLMENT	PELL GRANT RECIPIENTS (NUMBER)	PELL GRANT RECIPIENTS (PERCENTAGE)	NOTES
New College of the Univ. of South Florida, FL	629	—	—	1
Northwestern University, IL	9,167	870	9.5	
Pomona College, CA	1,548	186	12.0	
Princeton University, NJ	4,744	350	7.4	
Rice University, TX	2,728	341	12.5	
Stanford University, CA	7,279	855	11.7	
Swarthmore College, PA	1,467	191	13.0	
Tufts University, MA	4,775	498	10.4	
United States Air Force Academy, CO	4,365	—	—	2
United States Coast Guard Academy, CT	897	—	—	2
United States Military Academy, NY	4,152	—	—	2
United States Naval Academy, MD	4,297	—	—	2
University of Chicago, IL	4,075	507	12.4	
University of Notre Dame, IN	8,208	660	8.0	
University of Pennsylvania, PA	11,781	1,157	9.8	
University of Virginia, VA	13,764	1,183	8.6	
Vassar College, NY	2,439	291	11.9	
Wake Forest University, NC	4,136	289	7.0	
Washington and Lee University, VA	1,712	58	3.4	
Washington University in St. Louis, MO	6,772	544	8.0	
Webb Institute, NY	73	0	0.0	
Wellesley College, MA	2,273	355	15.6	
Wesleyan University, CT	2,792	385	13.8	
Williams College, MA	1,997	188	9.4	
Yale University, CT	5,286	536	10.1	

TABLE A.2 HIGHLY COMPETITIVE INSTITUTIONS

INSTITUTION	UNDER-GRADUATE ENROLLMENT	PELL GRANT RECIPIENTS (NUMBER)	PELL GRANT RECIPIENTS (PERCENTAGE)	NOTES
Austin College, TX	1,227	301	24.5	
Babson College, MA	1,719	166	9.7	
Beloit College, WI	1,273	203	15.9	
Boston University, MA	17,602	1,910	10.9	
Brandeis University, MA	3,081	417	13.5	
Brigham Young University, UT	29,815	9,188	30.8	
Bryn Mawr College, PA	1,333	197	14.8	
Bucknell University, PA	3,431	414	12.1	
Carleton College, MN	1,948	196	10.1	
Case Western Reserve University, OH	3,381	461	13.6	
College of the Atlantic, ME	269	71	26.4	
Colorado College, CO	1,934	324	16.8	
Colorado School of Mines, CO	2,952	411	13.9	
Connecticut College, CT	1,835	194	10.6	
Drew University/College of Liberal Arts, NJ	1,536	230	15.0	
Emory University, GA	6,374	776	12.2	
Franklin and Marshall College, PA	1,887	161	8.5	
Furman University, SC	2,767	238	8.6	
George Washington University, DC	10,063	903	9.0	
Gettysburg College, PA	2,277	275	12.1	
Grinnell College, IA	1,338	178	13.3	
Hamilton College, NY	1,755	260	14.8	
Hampshire College, MA	1,219	213	17.5	
Illinois Institute of Technology, IL	1,842	353	19.2	
Illinois Wesleyan University, IL	2,064	237	11.5	
Jewish Theological Seminary, NY	173	0	0.0	
Kenyon College, OH	1,587	131	8.3	
Kettering University, MI	2,653	460	17.3	

TABLE A.2 HIGHLY COMPETITIVE INSTITUTIONS, CONT.

Institution	Under-Graduate Enrollment	Pell Grant Recipients (Number)	Pell Grant Recipients (Percentage)	Notes
Knox College, IL	1,143	242	21.2	
Lafayette College, PA	2,330	175	7.5	
Lawrence University, WI	1,323	248	18.7	
Lehigh University, PA	4,650	581	12.5	
Loyola College in Maryland, MD	3,477	245	7.0	
Lyon College, AR	521	167	32.1	
Macalester College, MN	1,822	273	15.0	
Mary Washington College, VA	4,171	402	9.6	
Miami University, OH	19,329	2,839	14.7	
Mount Holyoke College, MA	2,037	424	20.8	
New York University, NY	19,028	3,509	18.4	
Oberlin College, OH	2,840	482	17.0	
Pennsylvania State University/ Univ. Park, PA	34,539	—	—	3
Pepperdine University, CA	2,936	516	17.6	
Pitzer College, CA	921	225	24.4	
Providence College, RI	4,341	366	8.4	
Reed College, OR	1,396	228	16.3	
Rhodes College, TN	1,535	150	9.8	
Rose-Hulman Institute of Technology, IN	1,573	233	14.8	
Rutgers University/College of Engineering, NJ	28,351	9,848	34.72	
Rutgers University/Cook College, NJ	—	—	—	4
Rutgers University/ Rutgers College, NJ	—	—	—	4
Saint Louis University, MO	9,604	1,400	14.6	
Saint Mary's College of Maryland, MD	1,688	196	11.6	
Saint Olaf College, MN	3,011	382	12.7	
Santa Clara University, CA	4,279	568	13.3	

Table A.2 Highly Competitive Institutions, cont.

Institution	Under- graduate Enrollment	Pell Grant Recipients (number)	Pell Grant Recipients (percentage)	Notes
Sarah Lawrence College, NY	1,214	151	12.4	
Scripps College, CA	798	112	14.0	
Skidmore College, NY	2,487	330	13.3	
Smith College, MA	2,665	642	24.1	
Southwestern University, TX	1,320	173	13.1	
State University of New York/ University at Binghamton, NY	10,167	—	—	5
State University of New York/ College at Geneseo, NY	5,371	—	—	5
State University of New York/ College of Environmental Science and Forestry, NY	1,193	—	—	5
Stevens Institute of Technology, NJ	1,655	388	23.4	
Syracuse University, NY	12,464	2,500	20.1	
The College of New Jersey, NJ	5,971	859	14.4	
Trinity College, CT	2,074	273	13.2	
Trinity University, TX	2,383	264	11.1	
Tulane University, LA	7,479	1,239	16.6	
Union College, NY	2,118	321	15.2	
United States Merchant Marine Academy, NY	850	—	—	6
University of California, Berkeley, CA	23,269	7,549	32.4	
University of California, Davis, CA	21,356	6,080	28.5	
University of California, Los Angeles, CA	25,328	8,887	35.1	
University of California, Santa Barbara, CA	17,724	4,395	24.8	
University of Florida, FL	33,639	7,384	22.0	
University of Georgia, GA	24,829	3,349	13.5	
University of Illinois at Urbana-Champaign, IL	28,746	4,483	15.6	

TABLE A.2 HIGHLY COMPETITIVE INSTITUTIONS, CONT.

INSTITUTION	UNDER-GRADUATE ENROLLMENT	PELL GRANT RECIPIENTS (NUMBER)	PELL GRANT RECIPIENTS (PERCENTAGE)	NOTES
University of Miami, FL	9,359	2,051	21.9	
University of Michigan, Ann Arbor, MI	24,547	3,073	12.5	
University of North Carolina at Chapel Hill, NC	15,844	2,090	13.2	
University of Puget Sound, WA	2,604	369	14.2	
University of Richmond, VA	3,663	186	5.1	
University of Rochester, NY	4,665	843	18.1	
University of Southern California, CA	16,037	3,868	24.1	
University of the South, TN	1,329	173	13.0	
University of Wisconsin-Madison, WI	29,861	3,484	11.7	
Ursinus College, PA	1,324	251	19.0	
Vanderbilt University, TN	6,077	609	10.0	
Villanova University, PA	7,392	635	8.6	
Wheaton College, IL	2,386	301	12.6	
Whitman College, WA	1,439	126	8.8	
Worcester Polytechnic Institute, MA	2,823	421	14.9	

NOTES:

1. The University of South Florida awards all Pell Grants centrally, so no separate data are available for New College.
2. The federal government provides full scholarships for all attendees.
3. Pennsylvania State University awards all Pell Grants centrally, so no separate data are available for the main University Park campus.
4. Enrollment and Pell Grant data are for all undergraduates at Rutgers.
5. The State University of New York awards all Pell Grants centrally, so no separate data are available for each campus.
6. The federal government provides full scholarships for all attendees.

SOURCES:

Undergraduate enrollment data were obtained from IPEDS College Opportunities On-Line, Integrated Postsecondary Education Data System, National Center for Education Statistics,

Continued

Sources (continued)

Washington, D.C., available online at http://nces.ed.gov/ipeds/cool/ and represent enrollments in the fall of the 2001–2002 academic year. The Pell Grant data for the same academic year were provided by Barry Goldstein of the Office of Federal Student Aid, U.S. Department of Education. Figures from the 1999–2000 National Postsecondary Student Aid Study were calculated from the Data Analysis System of the National Center for Education Statistics, Washington, D.C., available online at http://nces.ed.gov/das. Median income figures for the nation were obtained from the 2000 Census, U.S. Department of Commerce, Census Bureau, available online at http://www.census.gov/main/www/.

NOTES

INTRODUCTION

1. This finding is consistent with William G. Bowen and Derek Bok's study of twenty-eight selective colleges, reported in *The Shape of the River: Long-Term Consequences of Considering Race in College and University Admissions* (Princeton, N.J.: Princeton University Press, 1998). Bowen and Bok find that the bottom 28 percent by socioeconomic status have just a 3 percent representation at these selective colleges (see p. 341).

2. Dick Morris, *Behind the Oval Office: Getting Reelected against All Odds* (New York: Random House, 1998), p. 224.

3. Bridget Terry Long, "The Impact of Federal Tax Credits for Higher Education Expenses," NBER Working Paper no. w9553, National Bureau of Economic Research, Cambridge, Mass., March 2003, pp. 29–30.

4. Early admissions is on the rise, despite the recent decision of a few high-profile universities, like Yale and Stanford, to discontinue its use. See Karen W. Arenson, "Early Admissions Are Rising as Colleges Debate Practice," *New York Times,* December 23, 2002, p. A18. The decision by U.S. News and World Report to discontinue the practice of factoring acceptance "yield" into its annual rankings is not expected to alter the trend significantly. See Jacques Steinberg, "College Ratings by U.S. News Will Now Skip a Key Factor," *New York Times,* July 10, 2003, p. A14.

5. Federal aid to older students, who are financially independent, is pegged to personal rather than parental income.

6. Kenneth J. Cooper, "The Well-to-Do at the Public U.," *Washington Post,* November 25, 1999, p. A3.

7. Originally, ACT stood for American College Testing. In 1996, however, the organization shortened its name to ACT to reflect the broad array of programs and services beyond college entrance testing that it offers.

8. Carnevale and Rose find that at the 146 most selective colleges, if grades and test scores were the sole measure of admissions, the classes would be just 4 percent African American and Latino, even though those groups constitute 28 percent of eighteen-year-olds. This degree of underrepresentation would be comparable to the current underrepresentation of low-income students, who make up 3 percent of the population at selective colleges but 25 percent of eighteen-year-olds. For similar findings in Bowen and Bok's analysis, see the discussion in Richard D. Kahlenberg, "Style, Not Substance," *Washington Monthly,* November 1998, pp. 45–48.

9. For example, the editors of the *New York Times* argue that racial integration in higher education is especially important because elementary schools are segregated by race. But they make no comparable argument that economic integration in higher education is important, even though elementary schools also are segregated by economic class. See "Upholding Affirmative Action," *New York Times,* December 3, 2002, p. A30.

10. "Brief of Harvard University, Brown University, The University of Chicago, Dartmouth College, Duke University, The University of Pennsylvania, Princeton University, and Yale University as Amici Curiae Supporting Respondents," nos. 02-241 and 02-516, *Grutter v. Bollinger* and *Gratz v. Bollinger,* U.S. Supreme Court, p. 22, n. 13, available online at http://www.umich.edu/~urel/admissions/legal/gra_amicus-ussc/um/ Harvard-both.pdf.

11. Bowen and Bok, *Shape of the River,* p. 50.

12. Under a system of grades and test scores, the bottom 50 percent by income would have an 11 percent representation at the 146 most selective colleges they study. Under the current system of race-based affirmative action, the bottom half actually does marginally worse than it would under the system of grades and test scores, dropping to 10 percent.

13. Linda F. Wightman, "The Threat to Diversity in Legal Education: An Empirical Analysis of the Consequences of Abandoning Race as a Factor in Law School Admission Decisions," 72 *New York University Law Review* 42–43 (1997).

14. See, e.g., Daniel Golden, "Many Colleges Bend Rules to Admit Rich Applicants," *Wall Street Journal,* February 20, 2003, p. A1.

15. Carnevale and Rose acknowledge this is not the way colleges would or should admit individual students. A student with a 1280 combined SAT who is economically disadvantaged should have a greater (not an equal) shot at admissions than an economically privileged student scoring 1300. Likewise, at the other extreme, an economically disadvantaged student scoring 1000 should have a smaller (not an equal) chance of being admitted than a well-off student receiving a 1600. That is to say, in these examples, the preference for disadvantaged students should be more than twenty SAT points but less than six hundred points. However, these individual effects are

likely to cancel one another out, and, in approximating rough shares of students at the 146 colleges, Carnevale and Rose's simulation provides a fair and accurate aggregate prediction.

16. Thomas J. Kane, "Racial and Ethnic Preference in College Admissions," in Christopher Jencks and Meredith Phillips, eds., *The Black-White Test Score Gap* (Washington, D.C.: Brookings Institution Press, 1998), p. 432.

17. See Ethan Bronner, "Dividing Lines: Colleges Look for Answers to Racial Gap in Testing," *New York Times,* November 8, 1997, p. A1 (citing an unpublished dissertation by an author not named in the article at the Harvard Graduate School of Education).

18. Nicholas Lemann, *The Big Test: The Secret History of the American Meritocracy* (New York: Farrar, Straus and Giroux, 1999), p. 59.

19. *Gratz v. Bollinger*, 123 S. Ct. 2411, 2443 (2003).

20. Bowen and Bok, *Shape of the River,* p. 49, Figure 2.12.

21. See Derek Bok, quoted in Richard D. Kahlenberg, *The Remedy: Class, Race, and Affirmative Action* (New York: Basic Books, 1996), p. 29.

22. See Michael J. Sandel, *Liberalism and the Limits of Justice* (Cambridge: Cambridge University Press, 1982), pp. 141–42 (describing, though not endorsing, this view).

23. *Grutter v. Bollinger,* 2003 U.S. LEXIS 4800, *62 (2003).

24. "Comprehensive Review," Facts about the University of California, Office of Strategic Communications, University of California, November 2001.

25. E-mail correspondence from Tim Washburn, director of admissions, University of Washington, to author, December 2, 2002.

26. Joni James, "One Florida Remains Thorny," *Miami Herald,* October 28, 2002, p. A1. Profile assessment and the other portions of Florida's race-neutral efforts have proved more important to the overall goal of racial diversification at Florida's universities than has the much-vaunted plan to admit students from the top 20 percent of their classes. The "Talented 20" program, in fact, helped fewer than 1 percent of students admitted. See Patricia Marin and Edgar K. Lee, "Appearance and Reality in the Sunshine State: The Talented 20 Program in Florida," Civil Rights Project, Harvard University, 2003, pp. 21–22, available online at http://www.civilrightsproj ect.harvard.edu/research/affirmativeaction/florida.pdf.

27. See, e.g., Carol M. Swain, *The New White Nationalism in America: Its Challenge to Integration* (Cambridge: Cambridge University Press, 2002), pp. 192–97, 212, and 351–68; John David Skrentny, ed., *Color Lines: Affirmative Action, Immigration, and Civil Rights Options for America* (Chicago: University of Chicago Press, 2001), pp. 16–17 and 226–27; Sam Howe Verhovek, "In Poll, Americans Reject Means but Not Ends of Racial Diversity," *New York Times,* December 14, 1997, p. A1; Richard Morin,

"Misperceptions Cloud Whites' View of Blacks," *Washington Post*, July 11, 2001, p. A1.

28. EPIC/MRA poll (conducted January 29–February 3, 2003); *Los Angeles Times* poll (conducted January 30–February 2, 2003); *Newsweek* poll (conducted January 16–17, 2003).

29. See Skrentny, *Color Lines*, pp. 259 (Great Britain), 288 (France), and 307 (India).

30. Others, like Thomas Kane, predict even larger declines in racial diversity when economic affirmative action is employed. See Kane, "Racial and Ethnic Preference in College Admissions," pp. 448–51 (noting that, while blacks and Hispanics are disproportionately represented among low-income students, only 17.3 percent of high-scoring, low-income students are black and Hispanic). Carnevale and Rose appear to receive different results in part because they consider a pool of applicants in the top 25 percent of test takers, while Kane looks at the top 10 percent. In addition, while Kane looks at income as a proxy for disadvantage, Carnevale and Rose look at income, education, occupation, and high school economic status. Carnevale and Rose's methodology appears to be superior in both respects. The decision to reach deeper into the pool of test takers is closer to the practice employed in the use of racial affirmative action, for which Kane estimates the impact of being African American at four hundred SAT points. Likewise, an admissions officer would always want to look at more qualifications, not less, in considering applicants. Indeed, Carnevale and Rose's analysis could be improved by adding additional characteristics like net worth and neighborhood poverty concentrations (see discussion in text that follows).

31. See, e.g., Andrew Hacker, *Two Nations: Black and White, Separate, Hostile, Unequal* (New York: Charles Scribner's Sons, 1992), p. 146.

32. See Darly Fears, "Disparity Marks Black Ethnic Groups, Report Says," *Washington Post*, March 9, 2003, p. A7.

33. Edward N. Wolff, *Top Heavy: The Increasing Inequality of Wealth in America and What Can Be Done about It*, 2d ed. (New York: New Press, 2002), p. 20, Table 4.1.

34. Dalton Conley, "The Cost of Slavery," *New York Times*, February 15, 2003, p. A25.

35. Data provided to author for the entering class in fall 2002 by Andrea Sossin-Bergman, director of admissions, UCLA Law School, November 2002. African Americans constituted 17.1 percent of those admitted under the socioeconomic status program (19 of 111), compared with 1.5 percent of admissions for all other programs (13 of 848). Likewise, Latinos constituted 23.4 percent of socioeconomic status admissions (26 of 111), compared with 4.2 percent for other admissions (36 of 848). Even though the socioeconomic status program admitted 111 students, compared to 848 under other criteria, the absolute number of African Americans admitted

by dint of economic affirmative action (19) exceeded the number admitted under other programs (13).

The overall number of low-income and minority students enrolled at UCLA Law School remains relatively small because the law school admitted only 12 percent of its students through the socioeconomic status program. In addition, UCLA Law School faces an uneven playing field in recruiting minority applicants. UCLA's economic affirmative action program must compete for minority students who are being offered massive racial preferences at other law schools (private law schools in California and public and private law schools in most of the rest of the country) and may be courted with the offer of race-based scholarships. This problem is exacerbated because some minority students are particularly interested in attending a school with a strong core of minority classmates and do not even apply to the relatively few universities now operating under a ban on racial preferences. The racial dividend of economic affirmative action is likely to be much greater when all schools are playing by the same set of rules.

36. See Michael J. Puma et al., *Prospects: Final Report on Student Outcomes* (Cambridge, Mass.: Abt Associates, 1997), p. 12. (In a congressionally mandated study of grades one through nine the grade of "A" in high-poverty schools was equivalent to a grade of "C" in low-poverty schools when students were compared on standardized tests.)

37. Fred Hiatt, "Texas's 10 Percent Experiment," *Washington Post,* October 28, 2002, p. A19.

38. The University of Texas at Austin does not rank in the list of Barron's 146 top colleges, though it is included in the *U.S. News and World Report* top-fifty list. The university admits 64 percent of students, compared to a 26 percent acceptance rate at the University of California,. Berkeley. See Catherine L. Horn and Stella M. Flores, *Percent Plans in College Admissions: A Comperative Analysis of Three States' Experiences,* Civil Rights Project, Harvard University, February, 2003, available online at http:\www.civil rightsproject.harvard.edu\research\affirmativeaction\tristate.pdf..

CHAPTER 1

1. National Center for Education Statistics, *Digest of Education Statistics 2000* (Washington, D.C.: U.S. Department of Education, 2001), pp. 201–2, Tables 172 and 173, available online at http://nces.ed.gov/pubs2001/digest.

2. Ibid., p. 17, Table 8.

3. See *A Young Person's Guide to Learning and Earning,* Center for Education Policy and American Youth Policy Forum, Washington, D.C., 1998.

4. National Center for Education Statistics, *The Condition of Education 1997* (Washington, D.C.: U.S. Department of Education, 1997), p. 65, Indicator 9.

5. Michael S. McPherson and Morton O. Schapiro, "Changing Patterns of Institutional Aid," in Donald E. Heller, ed., *The Condition of Access: Higher Education for Lower Income Students* (Phoenix: American Council on Education and Oryx Press, 2002), Table 5.4. The authors use SAT score ranges to define institutional selectivity.

6. See *The Forgotten Half: Pathways to Success for America's Youth and Young Families,* Commission on Work, Family and Citizenship, William T. Grant Foundation, Washington, D.C., 1988; *The Forgotten Half Revisited,* American Youth Policy Forum, Washington, D.C., 1998.

7. For a recent analysis of what influences college opportunity and persistence in pursuing a course of study, especially for low-income students, see Patrick T. Terenzini, Alberto F. Cabrera, and Elena M. Bernal, *Swimming Against the Tide: The Poor in Higher Education* (New York: College Board, 2001).

8. Carnegie Commission on Higher Education, *Quality and Equality: New Levels of Federal Responsibility for Higher Education* (New York: McGraw-Hill, 1968); *Toward Equal Opportunity for Higher Education* (New York: College Board, 1973).

9. Martin Kramer, "Linking Access and Aspirations: The Dual Purpose of Pell Grants," in Lawrence E. Gladieux, ed., *Memory, Reason, Imagination: A Quarter Century of Pell Grants* (New York: College Board, 1998), pp. 32–41.

10. Arthur Levine and Jana Nidiffer, *Beating the Odds: How the Poor Get to College* (San Francisco: Jossey-Bass, 1996).

11. Thomas J. Kane, *The Price of Admission: Rethinking How Americans Pay for College* (Washington D.C.: Brookings Institution, 1999), p. 95.

12. Ibid., p. 101ff.

13. *Access Denied: Restoring the Nation's Commitment to Equal Educational Opportunity,* Advisory Committee on Student Financial Assistance, Washington, D.C., February 2001, pp. 10–11.

14. Ibid.

15. The comparison presented here between Pell Grants and federal student loans is based on aid available to students as a result of these programs, which in the case of loans is not the same as federal budget expenditures. By guaranteeing private bank loans through the Federal Family Education Loan Program (FFELP) and providing loan capital directly through the Ford Direct Student Loan Program (FDSLP), the federal government made it possible for students and parents to borrow $43 billion in 2000–2001, more than five times the $7.9 billion that Congress made available for Pell Grants in that year. While the cost to taxpayers is virtually 100

percent of each grant, the cost of repayable loans is much less, depending on interest rate conditions and defaults on repayment. The present-value estimate of cash flows for the cohort of loans in fiscal year 2000 was approximately $2 billion, including special allowances to lenders, in-school interest benefits to lenders on behalf of borrowers, and default insurance.

16. See Kramer, "Linking Access and Aspirations," pp. 32–41.

17. See Sarah E. Turner, "The Vision and Reality of Pell Grants: Unforeseen Consequences for Students and Institutions," in Gladieux, *Memory, Reason, Imagination,* pp. 49–65.

18. "Higher Education: Restructuring Student Aid Could Reduce Low-Income Student Dropout Rate," GAO/HRD-93-47, U.S. General Accounting Office, March 23, 1995.

19. *Trends in Student Aid 2001* (New York: College Board, 2001), p. 4.

20. Jacqueline E. King, *Crucial Choices: How Students' Financial Decisions Affect Their Academic Success* (Washington, D.C.: American Council on Education, 2002).

21. "Hope Scholarships" is a misnomer since it is actually a tax benefit.

22. *Taking Stock: How Americans Judge Quality, Affordability, and Leadership at U.S. Colleges and Universities,* American Council on Education, Washington, D.C., 2001.

23. National Commission on the Cost of Higher Education, *Straight Talk about College Costs and Prices* (Phoenix: Oryx Press, 1998), p. 12.

24. *Measuring Up 2000: The State-by-State Report Card for Higher Education,* National Center for Public Policy and Higher Education, San Jose, 2000.

25. National Center for Education Statistics, *Digest of Education Statistics 2000,* Table 328, p. 359.

26. See, for example, Michael S. McPherson and Morton O. Schapiro, *Keeping College Affordable: Government and Educational Opportunity* (Washington, D.C.: Brookings Institution, 1991).

27. Donald E. Heller, "State Student Aid," in Heller, *Condition of Access,* p. 63.

28. Ibid., p. 65.

29. College Savings Plans Network, *Special Report on State College Savings Plans 1998* (Lexington, Ky.: National Association of State Treasurers, 1998), may be ordered online at http://www.collegesav ings.org/cspn_products.htm.

30. Michael S. McPherson and Morton O. Schapiro, *The Student Aid Game: Meeting Need and Rewarding Talent in American Higher Education* (Princeton, N.J.: Princeton University Press, 1998), pp. 91–103.

31. Donald E. Heller, "Institutional Use of Need and Non-Need Financial Aid: What Can We Learn from NPSAS?" paper delivered at the 16th Annual NASSGAP/NCHELP Research Network Conference, Savannah, May 1999.

32. Anthony P. Carnevale and Richard A. Fry, *Crossing the Great Divide: Can We Achieve Equity When Generation Y Goes to College?* (Princeton, N.J.: Educational Testing Service, 2000), p. 13.

33. Samuel M. Kipp III, "Demographic Trends and Their Impact on the Future of the Pell Grant Program," in Gladieux, *Memory, Reason, Imagination,* pp. 109–32.

34. While the Bush administration has not called for elimination or reduction of tuition tax provisions, Deputy Secretary of Education William Hansen has signaled that the administration wants to take a broad approach to the upcoming reauthorization of the Higher Education Act, including aid programs authorized by other laws, such as college savings incentives and Hope Scholarships and the Lifetime Learning Tax Credit. See "ED: Even Tax Breaks in Play for HEA Amendments," *Education Daily*, December 4, 2001. Freeing up resources now spent on benefits administered through the tax code could conceivably boost chances of a major revitalization of Pell Grants and other need-based federal financial aid.

35. Lawrence E. Gladieux and Arthur M. Hauptman, eds., *The College Aid Quandary: Access, Quality, and the Federal Role* (Washington, D.C.: Brookings Institution, 1995), p. 49.

36. See *Ensuring Student Loan Repayment: A National Handbook of Best Practices* (Washington, D.C.: U.S. Department of Education, 2001), based on the Student Loan Repayment Symposium, Washington, D.C., October 2–4, 2000.

37. Michelle Miller-Adams, *Owning Up: Poverty, Assets, and the American Dream* (Washington, D.C.: Brookings Institution, 2002). See also Ray Boshara, "Poverty Is More than a Matter of Income," *New York Times*, September 29, 2002; the website of the New America Foundation, www.newamerica.net.

38. See King, *Crucial Choices,* p. 32.

CHAPTER 2

1. This chapter explores issues related to the preparation and performance of students who come from low-income families. What constitutes "low income" varies depending largely on available data. In most cases, low income refers either to students in the bottom income quartile or quintile or those with family incomes below a certain dollar level. The authors have tried to specify in each case what definition is being applied. In several instances data are not available by the family income of the student, and the authors have instead provided data by racial or ethnic minority status of the student to give a sense of the disparities.

2. It is not inconsistent for the United States to have average to below-average completion rates but high educational attainment compared to other

countries. The high participation rates in this country may be contributing to lower degree completion rates as more students "try" higher education while at the same time leading to high educational attainment measured as a percentage of the population receiving a degree.

3. National Center for Education Statistics, *Digest of Education Statistics 2000* (Washington, D.C.: U.S. Department of Education, page 339, Table 307, based on John Tuma, Sonya Geis, and C. Dennis Carroll, *High School and Beyond: 1992 Descriptive Summary of 1980 High School Sophomores 12 Years Later,* statistical analysis report, National Center for Education Statistics, U.S. Department of Education, January 1995, available online at http://nces.ed.gov/pubs95/95304.pdf.

4. In fiscal year 2002, GEAR-UP received an appropriation of $284 million, compared to an appropriation for Pell Grants alone of more than $11 billion (Budget of the U.S. Government, Fiscal Year 2004, Appendix, p. 335).

5. Thomas Mortenson, "Trends and Patterns in Higher Education Participation for Students from Low Income Families," testimony before the House Advisory Committee on Student Financial Assistance, U.S. Congress and U.S. Department of Education, April 12, 2000.

6. The scores of all test takers rose after the renorming of the SAT in the mid-1990s, but the gap remained as proportionately large as before the renorming. *Profile of College-Bound Seniors National Report,* College Board, New York, published annually.

7. "The Nation's Report Card: Reading," National Assessment of Educational Progress, National Center for Education Statistics, Washington, D.C., 2002, available online, http://nces.ed.gov/nationsreportcard/reading/results2002/lunch.asp.

8. National Center for Education Statistics, *Digest of Education Statistics 1998* (Washington, D.C.: U.S. Department of Education, 1999), Tables 131 and 133.

9. See Mark Berends and Daniel Koretz, "Identifying Students at Risk of Low Achievement in National Data," report no. MR-1006-ED, RAND Corporation, Santa Monica, Calif., June 1999, pp. viii–xi.

10. National Center for Education Statistics, *The Condition of Education, 2000* (Washington, D.C.: U.S. Department of Education, June 2000), indicator 30, available online at http://nces.ed.gov/programs/coe/2000pdf/30_2000.pdf.

11. See Peter Ewell, "Grading Student Learning: Better Luck Next Time," in *Measuring Up 2000: The State-by-State Report Card for Higher Education,* National Center for Public Policy and Higher Education, Wichita, 2001, available online at http://measuringup.highereducation.org/2000/pdf/commentary.pdf.

12. National Center for Education Statistics, *Digest of Education Statistics 2000*, Table 307.

13. Ibid.

14. A concomitant opportunity lies in the programs of research on teaching carried on by the faculty engaged in this training enterprise, but that topic is not addressed in depth in this paper.

15. See Suzanne M. Wilson, Robert E. Floden, and Joan Ferrini-Mundy, "Teacher Preparation Research: Current Knowledge, Gaps, and Recommendations," research report prepared for the U.S. Department of Education by the Center for Study of Teaching Policy, University of Washington, February 2001, available online at http://depts.washington.edu/ctpmail/PDFs/TeacherPrep-WFFM-02-2001.pdf; *What Matters Most: Teaching for America's Future,* Report of the National Commission on Teaching and America's Future, New York, September 1996, text available online at http://www.tc.columbia.edu/~teachcomm/WhatMattersMost.pdf; Harold Wenglinsky, "Teaching the Teachers: Different Setting, Different Results," Policy Information Report ED 446 138, Educational Testing Service, Princeton, N.J., August 2000, available online at http://www.ets.org/research/pic/tt.pdf; Dale Ballou and Michael Podgursky, "Reforming Teacher Preparation and Licensing: What Is the Evidence?" *Teachers College Record* (Columbia University) 102, no. 1 (Fall 2000): 5–27.

16. John I. Goodlad, *Teachers for Our Nation's Schools* (San Francisco: Jossey-Bass, 1990), pp. 290–92.

17. Gene Maeroff, Patrick M. Callan, and Michael D. Usdan, eds., *The Learning Connection: New Partnerships between Schools and Colleges* (New York: Teachers College Press, 2001); P. Michael Timpane and Lori S. White, eds., *Higher Education and School Reform* (San Francisco: Jossey-Bass, 1998).

18. "With Renewed Hope and Determination: A Statement by State Education CEOs, K–16," *Thinking K–16* (Education Trust, Washington, D.C.) 3, no. 2 (Fall 1999). See also Donald N. Langenberg and Nancy S. Shapiro, "K–16 in Maryland," *Basic Education* 46, no. 6 (February 2002), available online at http://www.c-b-e.org/be/iss0202/a1langenberg.htm.

19. Maeroff, Callan, and Usdan, *Learning Connection,* pp. 33–62.

20. The term TRIO refers to the three programs of Upward Bound, Talent Search, and Special Services that were enacted in the initial 1965 legislation. In the intervening years other programs such as Education Opportunity Centers have been added to the TRIO structure, but the TRIO designation remains.

21. The federal government in 2002 is distributing the results on a multiyear evaluation of some of the TRIO efforts.

22. See, for example, Arthur M. Hauptman, *The Tuition Dilemma: Assessing New Ways to Pay for College* (Washington, D.C.: Brookings Institution, 1990); Lawrence E. Gladieux and Watson Scott Swail, "Financial Aid Is Not Enough: Improving the Odds of College Success," *College Board*

Review, no. 185 (Summer 1998), reprint available online at http://www.educational policy.org/pdf/financial%20aid%20is%20not%20enough.pdf.

23. Hauptman, *Tuition Dilemma*, pp. 55–59.

24. U.S. Department of Education, Integrated Postsecondary Education Data System (IPEDS), as reported in National Center for Education Statistics, *Digest of Education Statistics 2002,* Table 330.

25. Sources for tuition and fee data include National Center for Education Statistics, *Digest of Education Statistics* published annually; "Trends in College Pricing," College Board, New York published annually; *AASCU 2001,* American Association of State Colleges and Universities, Washington, D.C., 2001.

26. The Current Population Survey, conducted by the Bureau of the Census every October, used to contain questions about the family income of college students who were categorized by type of institution, but this practice ended a number of years ago. One now must rely on periodic surveys such as the National Postsecondary Student Aid Survey for income distributions by type of institution. This is a far less satisfactory arrangement and is a good example of how data collection capacity in higher education in some ways has deteriorated sharply over the past several decades, despite the massive increase in the amount of government funds spent on data collection activitiesthe enterprise.

27. Kenneth S. Cooper, "The Well-to-Do of Public U.," *Washinton Post,* November 25, 1999, p. A3.

28. *AASCU 2001.*

29. National Center for Education Statistics, *Digest of Education Statistics 2000,* Tables 207, 223, and 224.

30. The National Center for Education Statistics regularly collects data on minority enrollments, but data collection on family income of students is less systematic. Occasional data sources on income distribution of college students include annual surveys of freshmen and periodic surveys of student aid recipients as part of the National Postsecondary Student Aid Survey (NPSAS).

31. David W. Breneman and Susan C. Nelson, *Financing Community Colleges: An Economic Perspective* (Washington, D.C.: Brookings Institution, 1981), Table 1–11.

32. National Center on Education Statistics, *Digest of Educational Statistics 2000,* Table 310, p. 341.

33. Ibid., Table 307. Data include all students who enroll in community colleges whether or not they expressed an intention or going on to a four-year program.

34. For an extensive discussion about community college transfer rates see Ellen M. Bradburn and David G. Hurst, "Community College Transfer Rates to 4-Year Institutions Using Alternative Definitions of Transfer,"

National Center for Education Statistics, U.S. Department of Education, 2001, available online at http://nces.ed.gov/pubs2002/quarterly/fall/q7-1.asp.

35. National Center for Education Statistics, *Digest of Education Statistics 2000,* Tables 223 and 265.

36. "Trends in Student Aid, 2001," College Board, New York, p. 6, Table 1, and p. 17, Table 10. State spending for aid was $4.6 billion in 2000–2001, while federal spending on aid was about $13 billion, including the GI Bill.

37. The best source on the trends in various forms of student aid relative to college costs is an annual publication of the College Board, "Trends in Student Aid," as referenced in the previous note.

38. For an analysis of the results of different student aid studies, see Larry L. Leslie and Paul T. Brinkman, *The Economic Value of Higher Education* (New York: Macmillan Publishing, 1988), Chapter 8.

39. Gary Orfield, "Money, Equity, and Access," *Harvard Educational Review,* Fall 1992, p. 337.

40. Adam Stoll and James B. Stedman, "Higher Education Tax Credits: Targeting, Value, and Interaction with Other Federal Student Aid," report no. RL31484, Congressional Research Service, July 2, 2002.

41. National Center for Education Statistics, *Digest of Education Statistics 2000,* Table 317, based on results from the National Postsecondary Student Aid Survey, 1995–96.

42. Stoll and Steadman, "Higher Education Tax Credits."

CHAPTER 3

1. Clifford Adelman, *Answers in the Tool Box: Academic Intensity, Attendance Patterns, and Bachelor's Degree Attainment,* U.S. Department of Education, June 1999, available online at http://www.ed.gov/pubs/Toolbox/index.html.

2. Test scores need to be put in some context because they do not measure all forms of "merit" and because of natural variation and luck. On the day of the exam, some students may have made correct "educated guesses" or been asked a series of questions that they were particularly familiar with. Conversely, other students made "bad guesses" or were asked about material that was outside their knowledge base. Throughout this report, we convert ACT scores into their SAT equivalent and report the data as "SAT-equivalent" scores.

3. Our analysis includes the 1995 freshman class at selective colleges. More recent analysis for the 1997 freshman class shows no change in the share of African American and Hispanic enrollment. More recent income data are not available, but trends in prices, admissions policy, and student aid policy suggest, ceteris paribus, that the share of low-income students at selective colleges should have gone down.

4. See Audrey Light and Wayne Strayer, "Determinants of College Completion: School Quality or Student Ability?" *Journal of Human Resources* 35, no. 2 (Spring 2000): 299–332. Light and Strayer also show that there is a higher graduation rate at more selective institutions. They argue, however, that the proper match between student ability and selectivity of the college is important: while better-qualified students have higher graduation rates at more selective institutions, the pattern is reversed for less qualified students, who graduate in higher proportions at nonelite colleges.

5. See William G. Bowen and Derek Bok, *The Shape of the River: Long-Term Consequences of Considering Race in College and University Admissions* (Princeton, N.J.: Princeton University Press, 1998), pp. 60–63. Bowen and Bok also document the relationship between SAT scoring and college graduation rates at the institutions that they studied. See also Nancy W. Burton and Leonard Ramist, *Predicting Success in College: SAT Studies of Classes Graduating since 1980,* College Board Report no. 2001-2, New York, College Board, 2001. Burton and Ramist provide an exhaustive survey of how SAT scores predict success in college.

6. The authors confirmed this using a probit analysis of the data: the coefficient on attending a top-tier college was positive and statistically significant even when a student's college entrance exam score and demographic background were included.

7. Adelman, *Answers in the Tool Box.*

8. See Bowen and Bok, *Shape of the River,* p. 107. Bowen and Bok document a similar relationship between college entrance exam score and the eventual pursuit of graduate school.

9. A probit analysis of this data shows that attending a top-tier college is a positive indicator for attending graduate school, even controlling for student background and ability. Dominic Brewer and colleagues find similar results. See Dominic J. Brewer, Eric Eide, and Ronald G. Ehrenberg, "Does It Pay to Attend an Elite Private College? Evidence on the Effects of Undergraduate College Quality on Graduate School Attendance," *Economics of Education Review* 17, no. 4 (October 1998): 371–76.

10. Robert G. Wood, Mary E. Corcoran, and Paul N. Courant, "Pay Differences among the Highly Paid: The Male-Female Earnings Gap in Lawyers' Salaries," *Journal of Labor Economics* 11, no. 3 (July 1993): 417–41.

11. Rachel Dunifon and Greg J. Duncan, "Long-Run Effects of Motivation on Labor Market Success," *Social Psychology Quarterly* 61, no. 1 (March 1998): 33–48.

12. John Cawley, James J. Heckman, and Edward Vytlacil, "Cognitive Ability and the Rising Return to Education," NBER Working Paper no. 6388, National Bureau of Economic Research, Cambridge, Mass., January 1998.

13. Robert A. Fitzgerald and Shelley Burns, *College Quality and the Earnings of Recent College Graduates,* Research Report no. NCES 2000–043, National Center for Education Statistics, U.S. Department of Education, August 2000, available online at http://nces.ed.gov/pubs2000 /2000043.pdf.

14. Ibid.

15. Thomas J. Kane, "Racial and Ethnic Preference in College Admissions," in Christopher Jencks and Meredith Phillips, eds., *The Black-White Test Score Gap* (Washington, D.C.: Brookings Institution Press, 1998)

16. Kermit Daniel, Dan Black, and Jeffery Smith, "College Quality and the Wages of Young Men," working paper (no. 9604001) available from Economics Working Paper Archive at WUSTL, Washington University, St. Louis, April 1996.

17. Stacy Berg Dale and Alan B. Krueger, "Estimating the Payoff to Attending a More Selective College: An Application of Selection on Observables and Unobservable," working paper no. 409, Industrial Relations Section, Princeton University, revised version, July 1999, available online at http://www.irs.princeton.edu/pubs/pdfs/409revised.pdf.

18. Brewer, Eide, and Ehrenberg, "Does It Pay to Attend an Elite Private College?"

19. Jere R. Behrman, Mark R. Rosenzweig, and Paul Taubman, "College Choice and Wages: Estimates Using Data on Female Twins," *Review of Economics and Statistics* 78, no. 4 (November 1996): 672–85.

20. Greg A. Perfetto, "Toward a Taxonomy of the Admissions Decision-Making Process," College Board, New York, 1999.

21. Hunter Breland et al., *Trends in College Admission 2000: A Report of a Survey of Undergraduate Admissions Policies, Practices, and Procedures,* sponsored by ACT, Inc., Association for Institutional Research, College Board, Educational Testing Service, and National Association for College Admission Counseling, 2000, summary report available online at http://air-web.org/images/trendssummary.pdf.

22. The complete survey has a margin of error of plus or minus three percentage points.

23. CBS/*New York Times* poll, December 6–9, 1997.

24. Based on an analysis of the 1996 National Election Study survey conducted by the Institute for Social Research at the University of Michigan.

25. *National Education Longitudinal Study 1988–1994, Descriptive Summary Report, with an Essay on Access and Choice in Postsecondary Education,* report no. NCES 96-175, National Center for Education Statistics, U.S. Department of Education, May 1996, available online at http://nces .ed.gov/pubs/96175.html.

26. In families with high expectations, 76 percent took the SAT or ACT, and 50 percent scored above 1000. In families with low expectations, only 28 percent took a college entrance exam, and 9 percent surpassed 1000.

27. This estimate of the share of families in the lowest SES quartile of test takers is probably too low. About 30 percent of the sample did not take the test. This group was heavily concentrated among the lowest-SES families, and, from other data, it is known that those who did not take the NELS test were least likely to graduate from high school and to have college aspirations.

28. Caroline M. Hoxby, "Peer Effects in the Classroom: Learning from Gender and Race Variation," NBER Working Paper no. w7867, National Bureau of Economic Research, Cambridge, Mass., August 2000; Eric A. Hanushek et al., "Does Peer Ability Affect Student Achievement?" NBER Working Paper no. 8502, National Bureau of Economic Research, Cambridge, Mass., October 2001.

29. The authors tried other metrics, such as low "school social capital" (measured by such concerns as the safety of the high school as well as by the teachers' interest in their students) and percentage going on to four-year colleges, and found similar results.

30. Richard D. Kahlenberg, *All Together Now: Creating Middle-Class Schools through Public School Choice* (Washington, D.C.: Brookings Institution Press, 2001), pp. 25–37.

31. John Powell, "Socioeconomic School Integration," *Poverty and Race* 10, no. 6 (November/December 2001): 6.

32. Glenn C. Loury, *The Anatomy of Racial Inequality* (Cambridge, Mass.: Harvard University Press, 2002).

33. Michael Walzer, *Thick and Thin: Moral Argument at Home and Abroad* (Notre Dame, Ind.: University of Notre Dame Press, 1994).

34. Loury, *Anatomy of Racial Inequality*, p. 166.

35. Ibid., p. 74.

36. "Access Denied: Restoring the Nation's Commitment to Equal Educational Opportunity," Report of the Advisory Committee on Student Financial Assistance, Washington, D.C., February 2001, available online at http://www.ed.gov/offices/AC/ACSFA/access_denied.pdf.

37. See Anthony P. Carnevale, Richard Fry, and Sarah Turner, "Against the Odds . . . Is College Graduation Declining for Low-Income Youth?" Leadership 2000 Series, Educational Testing Service, Princeton, N.J., forthcoming. These findings are confirmed in another study performed by ETS using a different data set—the Panel Study of Income Dynamics. Controlling for other background circumstances, about six out of every ten adolescents from families with incomes in excess of $65,000 will complete at least one year of college before age twenty-five, while only one-third from families with incomes of less than $30,000 will do so. Roughly 40 percent of higher-income students will achieve bachelor's degrees, compared with 13 percent of students from lower-income families. The share of students who complete a year of college or get a bachelor's degree has risen among both high- and low-income students since the 1970s, but the gap has remained the same.

38. See Bowen and Bok, *Shape of the River*, p. 27. Bowen and Bok use a unique data set from twenty-eight elite colleges and find that only two-thirds of white applicants with SAT-equivalent scores greater than 1500 are offered admission.

39. Michael T. Nettles, Catherine Millet, Marne K. Einarson, University of Michigan, "A Hierarchical Model of Influence on College Admissions Test Performance," presentation at the 41st Annual AIR Forum, June 5, 2001.

40. Other studies tend to confirm this result. For instance, in "Statistics in Brief: Making the Cut: Who Meets Highly Selective College Entrance Criteria?" report no. NCES 95-732, National Center for Education Statistics, U.S. Department of Education, April 1995, available online at http://nces .ed.gov/pubs/95732.html, the NCES performed a similar exercise. Using criteria of GPA>3.5, SAT-equivalent score>1200, core courses in basic English, math, and science, strong teacher recommendations, and participation in at least two extracurricular activities, the researchers found that only 0.4 percent of blacks versus 6.5 percent of whites met all the qualifications. Using these criteria, African Americans would make up 1 percent of the applicant pool for selective college admissions.

41. For discussion of lotteries, see, e.g., Susan Sturm and Lani Guinier, The Future of Affirmative Action: Reclaiming the Innovative Ideal, 84 *California Law Review* 953 (1996); Paul D. Berger, Chen Wang, and James P. Monahan, "Quantifying a Statistical Aspect of Segmented Selection/ Quota Systems," *American Statistician* 52, no. 3 (August 1998): 228–32; Richard Cohen, "'Bounding' of Test Scores as a Merit-Based Remedy for Employment Discrimination," remarks at Joyce Foundation conference on "The Civil Rights Act of 1964 in Perspective," National Judicial Center, Washington, D.C., November 1994; Bernard Grofman and Samuel Merrill, "Lottery-Based Affirmative Action in Education: Anticipating Likely Consequences," unpublished paper supported in part by the Program in Methodology, Measurement and Statistics, National Science Foundation, Washington, D.C., February 21, 2000, available online at http://hypatia.ss .uci.edu/ps/personnel/grofman/Lottery-Based.pdf.

42. See, e.g., Richard D. Kahlenberg, "In Search of Fairness: A Better Way," *Washington Monthly*, June 1998, pp. 26–30.

43. *Newsweek, Los Angeles Times,* and EPIC/MRA polls.

44. The use of wealth and concentrations of neighborhood poverty are likely to be particularly beneficial to African Americans.

Appendix

1. The author wishes to acknowledge the research assistance of Kimberly Rogers in compiling the data for this report.

2. This list of 146 colleges corresponds with those studied in the chapter of this volume by Anthony P. Carnevale and Stephen J. Rose, "Socio-economic Status, Race/Ethnicity, and Selective College Admissions."

3. Community colleges enroll relatively few dependent students who take enough courses to qualify for a Pell Grant; thus, the overall rate of Pell Grant awards drops when community colleges are included in the sample. If the sample is restricted to full-time dependents at four-year institutions and community colleges, the proportion of Pell Grant recipients among all students increases to 21 percent.

4. Approximately 47 percent of all Pell Grant recipients in four-year institutions are independent students. For federal financial aid purposes, a student can be declared independent if he or she meets one or more of the following conditions: is at least twenty-four years old; is married; is a veteran of the U.S. armed forces; has a dependent other than a spouse; or is an orphan.

INDEX

ABOUT THE CONTRIBUTORS

ANTHONY P. CARNEVALE, vice president for assessments, equity, and careers at Educational Testing Service, is an internationally recognized authority on education, training, and employment. He was appointed by President Clinton as a commissioner to the White House Advisory Committee on Technology and Adult Education and Training (which now serves under the direction of President Bush) and as chair of the National Commission for Employment Policy, while serving as vice president and director of human resource studies at the Committee for Economic Development. Earlier, he had been president of the Institute for Workbased Learning, an applied research center affiliated with the American Society for Training and Development. He has held senior staff positions in the U.S. Senate and House of Representatives and the U.S. Department of Health, Education, and Welfare. He was director of legislative affairs for the American Federation of State, County, and Municipal Employees (AFSCME). He coauthored the principal affidavit in *Rodriguez v. San Antonio*, a landmark U.S. Supreme Court action to remedy unequal tax burdens and educational benefits; this landmark case sparked significant educational equity reforms in a majority of states.

LAWRENCE E. GLADIEUX is an independent consultant whose clients have included the National Center for Public Policy and Higher Education, the James Irvine Foundation, the Advisory Committee on Student Financial Assistance, the American Federation of Teachers, and the U.S. Department of Education. From 1981 to 2000 he served as Washington representative and policy director for the College Board. He is editor of *Radical Reform or Incremental Change? Student Loan Policy Alternatives for the Federal Government* (Henry

Holt and Co., 1989) and coauthor (with Thomas R. Wolanin) of *Congress and the Colleges: The National Politics of Higher Education* (Lexington Books, 1976).

ARTHUR M. HAUPTMAN has been an independent public policy consultant and author since 1981. He is an internationally recognized expert and has written extensively on issues relating to student aid, college costs, and higher education finance generally. In the United States, he has consulted with many federal and state agencies, colleges and universities, and associations on policy issues relating to higher education. Internationally, he has worked with governmental and institutional officials in more than a dozen countries to help develop higher education financing strategies.

DONALD E. HELLER is associate professor and senior research associate at the Center for the Study of Higher Education at The Pennsylvania State University. Before coming to Penn State, he was a faculty member at the University of Michigan School of Education. He received the 2002 Promising Scholar/Early Career Achievement Award from the Association for the Study of Higher Education and was also the recipient in 2001 of the Robert P. Huff Golden Quill Award from the National Association of Student Financial Aid Administrators for his contributions to the literature on student financial aid. He is the editor of *The States and Public Higher Education Policy: Affordability, Access, and Accountability* (Johns Hopkins University Press, 2001) and *Condition of Access: Higher Education for Lower Income Students* (ACE/Praeger, 2002).

RICHARD D. KAHLENBERG, a senior fellow at The Century Foundation, is the author of *All Together Now: Creating Middle Class Schools through Public School Choice* (Brookings Institution Press, 2001), *The Remedy: Class, Race, and Affirmative Action* (Basic Books, 1996); and *Broken Contract: A Memoir of Harvard Law School* (Hill & Wang/Farrar, Straus & Giroux, 1992). He also is the editor of *Public School Choice vs. Private School Vouchers* (The Century Foundation Press, 2003) and *A Notion at Risk: Preserving Public Education as an Engine for Social Mobility* (The Century Foundation Press, 2000), and he facilitated the task force that produced *Divided We Fail: Coming Together through Public School*

Choice: The Report of The Century Foundation Task Force on the Common School (The Century Foundation Press, 2002). He is currently working on a biography of educator Albert Shanker.

STEPHEN J. ROSE is a Senior Research Economist at ORC Macro, a research and survey firm, where he leads their multiyear evaluation of adult basic education for the U.S. Department of Education. Prior to working with Macro, he worked for the Education Testing Service, the Department of Labor (as a senior advisor to Secretary Robert Reich), the National Commission on Employment Policy, the Joint Economic Committee of Congress, and the Ways and Means Committee of the Washington State Senate. He is the author of *Social Stratification in the United States,* 5th ed. (The New Press, 1999).

P. MICHAEL TIMPANE helps direct the Aspen Institute's program on education and society, serves as senior adviser for education policy for the RAND Corporation, and serves as an adviser to the Carnegie Corporation's Teachers for a New Era Intitiative. He is former president of Teachers College, Columbia University; former vice president and senior scholar at the Carnegie Foundation for the Advancement of Teaching; and former director of the federal government's National Institute of Education. He has published numerous articles and has coauthored or edited ten books and monographs on education and social policy, including *Rediscovering the Democratic Principles of Education* (University Press of Kansas, 2000).